D0436292

ALSO BY COLIN McGINN

Mindsight: Image, Dream, Meaning

Consciousness and Its Objects

The Making of a Philosopher:
My Journey Through Twentieth-Century Philosophy

Knowledge and Reality

The Mysterious Flame: Conscious Minds in a Material World

THE POWER OF MOVIES

THE POWER OF MOVIES

How Screen and Mind Interact

COLIN McGINN

Pantheon Books, New York

 Published in the United States by Pantheon Books, a division of Random House, Inc., New York, and in Canada by Random House of Canada Limited, Toronto.

Pantheon Books and colophon are registered trademarks of Random House, Inc.

Library of Congress Cataloging-in-Publication Data

McGinn, Colin, [date]
The power of movies : how screen and mind interact / Colin McGinn.
p. cm.
Includes bibliographical references.
ISBN 0-375-42317-6
1. Motion pictures—Psychological aspects. I. Title.

PN1995.M3785 2005
791.43'01'9—dc22 2005043049

www.pantheonbooks.com

Printed in the United States of America
First Edition
2 4 6 8 9 7 5 3 1

CONTENTS

PREFACE

Everyone enjoys a good film. But we seldom pause to ask ourselves what it is about film that makes it so appealing. What is it about film, with its distinctive form and methods, which accounts for its allure? This book is an attempt to answer that question.

The question came to my attention several years ago, when I was visiting New Orleans to give a lecture on dreams and the imagination (the steaminess seemed conducive). I had been working with the idea that our immersion in our dreams is analogous to the immersion we experience in fictional works, especially films. The idea was that our assent to what we dream might be a special case of our propensity to become involved in fictional products, allowing them to take over our minds—dream belief as fictional absorption. But then it occurred to me that perhaps the direction of illumination goes the other way too: maybe our experience of films is conditioned by our prior experience with dreams. Could it be that the allure of film is explained by the fact that films evoke the dreaming mind of the viewer? So began my inquiries into the nature of film and the way it is received by the viewing consciousness.

I soon learned that the dream interpretation of film has a history, with theorists of film sometimes mentioning the analogy. But the idea had never been fully developed and treated as a theory to be argued for and tested. Furthermore, other aspects of the film experience began to occur to me, notably the particular way in which we visually apprehend the screen, as well as the significance of the physical film image itself. Putting these ideas together is what this book is all about. I intend it for anyone interested in understanding his or her own response to cinema, as well as for people more professionally involved in movies—film students, critics, filmmakers, theorists of art. This is a subject in which analysis and theory can reveal unsuspected meanings, and I venture to suggest that grasping these meanings can change the way you watch movies. Reflective understanding of our spontaneous response to film images cannot help informing that response.

Working on this book involved the interplay between thinking theoretically about film and actually going to see movies. This is an agreeable way to work. Instead of feeling guilty about indulging my movie habit (sometimes in the afternoon!) I could regard it as serious research. Oh, I have labored long and hard in the movie theatres of the world. I invite my readers to do the same: read this book, then go to the movies, and see how the two mesh. The test is whether your movie experience is enriched.

My conversations with other movie enthusiasts have been very helpful, as I tried to probe their responses to film. I want to thank in particular Jonathan Miller, Oliver Sacks, Peter Kivy, Connor Martin, and Catherine Mortenson. I am also grateful to my agent, Susan Rabiner, and my editor, Dan Frank, both of whom made valiant efforts to save me from the pedantries characteristic of my calling (academic philosopher).

THE POWER OF MOVIES

One

THE POWER OF FILM

THE MIND-MOVIE PROBLEM

The power of film is indisputable. Since the beginning of movies, a little over a hundred years ago, they have captivated audiences. We want, badly, to watch. And this power seems unique to film. As the philosopher Stanley Cavell remarks, in *The World Viewed,* "the sheer *power* of film is unlike the powers of the other arts."[1] There is something about movies specifically—whether they emanate from America or France, Britain or Sweden—which succeeds in connecting to the human psyche in a deep way. Movies carry some sort of psychic charge that no other art form—perhaps no other spectacle—can quite match.

Their power is manifested in two ways: demographically and individually. Movies simply have a larger mass appeal than any other artistic medium. Nothing draws crowds in the millions like a new movie—and this was so from the very beginning. (It is this fact that explains the colossal investment of money that goes into the movie business. What would the movie industry be like today if movies had the demographics of, say, opera or stamp collecting?) People read novels and go to the theatre, of course, but it is the cinema that really packs them in. And this mass appeal is remarkably cross-cultural. All across the world people flock to the movies, and it is amazing how easy it is for a movie from one country to cross boundaries into another, perhaps with suitable subtitles or dubbing—I once watched a Clint Eastwood cowboy film in Paris in which the tough gunslinger intoned the words "Fermez la porte" in an impeccable French accent.

There is also, at the individual level, the *quality* of the attraction—the sheer intensity of the movie-watching experience. From childhood on, we are all familiar with that sense of entrancement that accompanies sitting quietly in the pierced darkness of the movie theatre. The mind seems to step into another sphere of engagement as the images on the screen flood into our receptive consciousness. We are *gripped*. The quality of this mental engagement, the way the mind is invaded and commandeered, is something that has been evident since the early days of the silent era, when film was at its least technologically sophisticated. The moving image itself seems an object of extraordinary potency. In the movie-watching experience we enter an "altered state of consciousness," enthralling and irresistible.

What *is* it about movies that explains their amazing hold over the human mind? Why do we love movies (and we do *love* them—thrill to their presence, romanticize them, suffer when they let us down)? Clearly, there must be something about those light projections through celluloid, on the one hand, and the nature of the human mind, on the other, that accounts for the seemingly preordained match that exists between them. How do they manage to mesh so naturally, smoothly, and overwhelmingly? I like to call this the "mind-movie problem," by analogy with the philosophical mind-body problem.[2] The mind-body problem is the problem of explaining how conscious experience relates to the physical materials of the body and brain; the mind-movie problem is the problem of explaining how it is that the two-dimensional moving image, as we experience it in a typical feature film, manages to hook our consciousness in the way it does. How do these jumpy splashes of light contrive to strike our mind with such force? Somehow movies and the mind are *suited* to one another, mutually adapted—and I want to explain what it is about both terms of this nexus that makes it as charged as it is. What is it about the screen image and the mind that views it that makes the marriage between them so successful—so passionate and tempestuous, one might almost say? What is this love affair with the screen?

DUBIOUS SUGGESTIONS

What accounts for the power of film? An obvious first thought is that movies are uniquely *realistic*—they recreate or reproduce the very events that they record. The camera, in this view, is a device for making available, for later consumption, the very same worldly events that took place before it at some earlier time. Accordingly, what we see in the movies is indistinguishable from what we would have seen had we been there at the original shooting. Suppose you would like to see what some historical battle actually looked like to a living onlooker; well, movies enable you to have this experience without having to travel back in time and witness the events themselves or have before you armies of real actors. Movies literally recreate worldly events before our very eyes. They duplicate reality. Seeing film is just like seeing the reality filmed. And reality certainly has the power to hold our attention.

This view is inadequate for a couple of reasons. It is simply not true that the movie image literally reproduces real events. We are never *fooled* by a movie depiction of a battle into thinking that we are really there—or else we might head smartly for the exit. A movie is not some kind of *illusion* of reality, if that means something that appears just like reality itself but isn't. We never really mistake a movie image for a real object, as if thinking that Harrison Ford, say, is in the theatre with us, feet away. The power of movies cannot be identical to the power of seeing the real events; the movie's power must lie in what *distinguishes* it from seeing real events. The power of seeing a real battle is just a different *kind* of power from that of seeing a movie of a battle (though that is not to say that the first kind of power is totally irrelevant to the second). Similarly, we can readily distinguish the stage in the performance of a play from the real world, not somehow confusing the events of the play with real events. We can likewise distinguish the screen in a movie theatre from a chunk of real reality (so to speak), not taking the images before us literally to be real objects and situations. The power of cinema does not derive from its giving us the full-blown illusion of reality—as when I might actually hallucinate the presence of a monster and be genuinely afraid, having taken the illusion to be reality. It is not that in a horror film, say, I am under the impression that a living (or unliving) vampire is literally standing not ten feet in front of me, and find myself understandably riveted; I know very well that it's just a *picture* of a vampire. And yet I am still riveted (though in a different way).

Nor do we find movies fascinating precisely in proportion to how fascinating we find reality. Reality itself might leave us bored and indifferent, but when it comes to us in the form of a movie image it can take on life and meaning. Watching someone light a cigarette in real life can be pretty dull, but in the context of a story projected onto the movie screen our eyes and mind will be drawn in. The movie *adds* something to reality, and this is part of its power (later we will explore in detail what exactly it adds). It is the same with painting: the interest of a portrait is very different from the interest we take in its sitter, who may be quite uninteresting to look at. The visual arts are not in general attempts to produce *twins* of real people. It is not the alleged *lifelikeness* of cinema that determines its interest for us, since (a) it is not lifelike in any literal sense, and (b) being lifelike is not enough to confer fascination on something. In short, the psychological power of a representation of something is not the same as the psychological power of that thing. Art, in other words, is transformative.

A different suggestion might be that movies engage our mind, not by simulating reality, but by offering us fiction. We love stories in general, and movies tell us stories in visual images instead of words on the page. Does our taste for fictional narratives explain our liking for movie narratives? We are quite aware that it is all just fiction; but fiction is what we crave, not quotidian reality. What moves us at the movie theatre is the power of the imagination.

Now it is certainly true that the fictional content of films must be part of their appeal—we like to get caught up in a good yarn—but this suggestion suffers from not specifying what it is about movies *in particular* that grips us so. What is it about films, as opposed to novels, that gives rise to our special engagement with them? It isn't just the story being told—indeed, we might find the story banal if it came to us in merely verbal form—it is the *form* in which the story comes to us that enthralls us. It is the fact that it is a story *on film* that creates the special power of cinema, not simply being a story told in some medium or other. If it were just the latter, then we might well prefer to stay home and read a book—which would be easier and cheaper. But what we crave when we itch to see a film is the particular nature of the cinematic experience—which includes, but is not exhausted by, the embedded narrative itself. Clearly, the experience of seeing photographic images on a screen is very different from seeing or hearing words that describe the selfsame events. We need to identify what specific properties of film contribute to the movie-watching experience. Obviously, seeing a film is not the same as hearing someone tell you the story of it!

It might be maintained that it is the *ideological* content of cinema that explains its sway over the minds of the audience. The movies, it is said, support and reinforce the prevailing ideology of the society within which they are made and viewed, and the population has already been brainwashed by this ideology into being mesmerized by the cinema's own version of it. The movies thus collude with the prevailing ideology, which has already wormed its way into the deeper layers of the audience's psyche. For example, a romantic comedy might reinforce sexual stereotypes, connecting with the attitudes already present in the audience. The power of cinema is thus the power of ideology.[3]

I would not wish to deny that movies can harbor ideological assumptions and biases—as any other art form can—and that these might well reflect and bolster similar assumptions and biases in the mind of a viewer. But this is not a very convincing account of the power of cinema. First, we again have nothing here to explain what is *distinctive* of film. Ideology can be foisted on people in any number of forms—speeches, advertising, literary fiction, jokes, even music—but cinema has a special kind of power for the viewer. I might find the ideology embedded in a film crude and unconvincing (for some reason the Rambo films come to mind); but the film might still engage my attention in powerful ways, because of something about film itself, as distinct from whatever ideology it might contain. Contrariwise, a film might conform to my ideological beliefs perfectly while leaving me cold. Secondly, surely it is possible for a film to embody no particular political ideology and still be a powerful viewing experience. What is the ideology of *The Wizard of Oz:* socialist, capitalist, colonialist, anti-witch, animal liberationist? Not everything is an exercise in power politics. So it can't be that the power of film derives from its consonance with the ideology people bring with them to the cinema. The filmic is simply not always the political. At a minimum, the power of film must have something essentially to do with the fact that films consist of *moving pictures,* not with the ideological baggage such pictures may or may not bring with them. (Or is there an implicit ideology even there—keep on the move, never rest, become two-dimensional!?)

This may prompt an appealingly straightforward response to our question—namely, people like moving pictures because they like to see movement depicted. The world around us consists of objects in motion, particularly human bodies, and what cinema achieves, in contradistinction to still photography, is precisely the depiction of movement. Isn't this why, at the dawn of cinema, people were so impressed by the new medium, in contrast to painting and photography? Movement itself can seem like the universe's most basic miracle. Imagine a totally static universe that clicked into animation after a few billion years of nothing: the new movement would seem astonishing. What cinema achieves is the manmade reproduction of the magic of movement. Like dance, movies celebrate the manifold ways of going from A to B. Moreover, not only can we reproduce the movement of things in a new form; we can also study and appreciate this movement better, by means of the close-up, slow motion, speed motion, and so on.

This theory has the advantage of drawing upon a distinctive property of the film medium—namely, that it consists of moving pictures—but it seems to me far too superficial to explain what needs to be explained. To be sure, we like to perceive movement in nature, but how much interest is there in watching a simple movement repeat itself, even a complex sequence of movements? Also, to go back to an earlier point, in watching filmed movement the viewer does not somehow mistake what she sees for the actual movement of objects—we are not under the illusion that objects are moving in front of us. Perhaps without movement movies would not strongly engage us, but movement by itself is not enough to account for the hold that movies have over the mind. The emotional resonance of film is entirely overlooked in this account. There was the charm of novelty when the moving image first came on the scene, but mere representations of movement would be a novelty that quickly wore off if there were nothing more to movies than that.

Those steeped in the ways of Freudian psychoanalysis may try a very different angle: movies engage the mind because they make subliminal contact with the unconscious mind. Movies filter down into the unconscious, where they meet up with our primitive repressed desires and childhood memories. Thus it has been suggested that the screen stands for the breast as a Freudian symbol, so that the film viewer is regressing to an infantile state in which he has still not differentiated himself from the objective world, and in which he still is attached to the all-encompassing mother. The attractions of the screen mimic the comforts of the breast.[4]

It is hard to discuss such proposals without undertaking a full-scale discussion of Freudian theory, which I cannot do here; but I take it few people will be immediately swayed by such farfetched ideas. As the film theorist Noël Carroll remarks, if the screen is the breast, where is the nipple?[5] Also, screens are flat, whereas breasts tend not to be—not to mention square and unitary. Perhaps there are unconscious fears and desires that some movies succeed in reaching, thus delivering to the viewer a psychic depth charge; but surely many movies have nothing to do with any supposed Freudian unconscious. It can hardly be that every movie plays out some Oedipal drama that pricks the viewer's unconscious. And, once again, the fact, if it is one, that certain narrative themes might mesh with the apparatus of Freudian psychology does nothing to explain what it is about movies specifically—as opposed to novels, theatre, painting, and so on—that engages us. If this were the correct explanation, then it would be hard to see why movies should stand out from these other media, quantitatively or qualitatively. Why should what is peculiarly cinematic connect so powerfully with Freudian psychical formations?

A final proposal—one made by Carroll, an astute commentator on the workings of film—is that movies offer us, by means of their cinematic devices, an unusually clear and intelligible medium.[6] We do not need to learn to watch films (unlike reading), and such devices as the close-up and variable framing (moving the camera around to produce different perspectives) serve to direct the viewer's attention to precisely where it needs to go in order the follow the action. Thus movies are uniquely accessible to the viewing mind—easily digested. While I would agree that movies do enjoy this kind of narrative perspicuity, this doesn't explain their power. Something can be easy to follow and yet profoundly boring. Why should the fact that I find something highly intelligible by itself make me enthralled by it? The impact on the psyche seems to go deeper than simply ease of processing. Carroll wants to suggest that the power of movies is a matter of how they are processed by the intellect. But isn't that power primarily manifested in the emotions generated by film? We need to know how movies tap so readily into our emotions, not merely how they are cognitively accessible. For movies to have their power, it is perhaps necessary that they be readily intelligible to the audience (though some affecting films are quite puzzling); but this does not seem sufficient to explain the peculiar power that they have. It is far too general a property to do that, possessed by many other art forms to one degree or another. We need to find something *unique* to film, not something that comes in degrees and can be possessed by other media. When I am mesmerized by a scene in a film, it is not simply because I *understand* it extremely well.

MOVIES AND PLAYS

When movies began, many people felt that this new medium was doomed, nothing more than a wan simulacrum of live theatre. Instead of live actors performing in front of you, in full 3-D with natural color and sound, the cinema offered only mute 2-D monochrome—a paltry substitute for the real thing. Once the novelty wore off, audiences would dwindle, and film would retire to its true calling—as a documentary medium, perhaps especially well suited to medical education. This prediction, of course, has been spectacularly refuted. But it enables us to frame our question in a sharp way: how does cinema differ from theatre in its ability to engage the mind? Both are visual media primarily (unlike the novel), and both involve the temporal sequencing of human actions (unlike painting); so what does cinema have that theatre lacks? It is easy to see what theatre has that cinema lacks—real performers in close proximity to the audience—but what is it that cinema gives us that theatre does not? How exactly is the movie experience unlike the theatre experience, and in ways that add to its appeal? That is how I shall be framing the question, so nothing can count as a good answer to it that fails to differentiate movies from stage plays. Throughout this book, then, I shall be concerned with what is peculiar to film—that is, peculiar to the psychology of film watching. I want to understand how movies work on the mind in virtue of their specific properties, and what it is about the mind that prepares it for the influence of movies. This is an investigation into the psychology of film—specifically, film reception. I shall be concerned with this question from the perceptual, cognitive, and affective viewpoints: how we *see* films, what the film image *means* to us, and how our *feelings* are aroused by film. Movies engage our psychological faculties in profound and unique ways. Though movies are of relatively recent origin, they call upon ancient and deep-seated aspects of the mind; and they enjoy significant liaisons with other aspects of our experience of the world. They serve to condense much of significance into a relatively brief and isolated experience—the experience of watching a movie.

Two

VISION AND THE SCREEN

LOOKING AND SEEING

You are sitting in the movie theatre, eyes turned toward the screen. Light images are being projected onto that blank expanse—a series of stills in very quick succession, seen as movement—and these images in turn project light into your eyes. You see something. You visually attend. There is an act of looking. But what do you see, what do you attend to, what do you look at? What, in general, is your visual relation to the screen, the moving image, the actors, the characters they play? For all of these things are distinct from each other: the screen isn't the image temporarily falling upon it; the image isn't identical to the actor whose image it is; and the actor cannot be identified (literally) with the character he or she plays. So what is your visual relation to each of these entities? When, as we say, we "watch a movie," what is going on with our eyes—with our whole visual system? This is the first stage at which the movie exerts its power over us—how it enters our eyes—and we need to know what kind of vision this involves.

It is clear enough that we *see* the images on the screen—those projected patterns of light. Our visual awareness represents those images, just as it does ordinary objects of sight. The images are patches of light that appear in visual consciousness, just as sunlight falling across the screen would be seen. It is less clear that we see the screen onto which the images are projected, at least once the movie starts. Before the movie starts, when the screen is blank, it can of course be readily seen (so long as the curtain is not in the way): it is just a large expanse of whitish gray right in front of you. But once the images start to inhabit its surface, it effectively disappears, covered up by the images. You certainly can't see its gray coloring. It is as if it has been covered with a coat of paint, rendering invisible what was once visible. (Television is different: here you see the screen even when the set is on, because the TV images are not thrown *onto* the screen.) The images themselves are what now occupy the visual field—they are straightforwardly seen. At best, the screen is seen in a secondary sense, as what "contains" the images.

But are the images that we see also *looked at*? We appear to be looking at *something* as we watch a movie—is it simply the images on the screen? I don't mean "look at" in the sense of "look toward"—the viewer's eyes are certainly oriented in the *direction* of the image—but in the sense of *attending* to them: Are we looking at them in the way we might be looking at the flaws in a piece of china or the petals on a flower—examining them, scrutinizing them, focusing on them? Are they the prime objects of our visual attention? This question has not been settled once we have decided whether the images are *seen,* since it is possible to see something you are not attending to or looking at. I might be searching for you in a crowd, but "look right through you": you certainly occupy my visual field and are seen by me, but

I don't focus on you or single you out from everyone else. At any given moment we are seeing a great many things, only some of which we are actively looking at or attending to. So are the images on the screen something we see but don't look at?

I think the answer is clearly yes. We are *not* attending to those patterns of light that we are no doubt seeing; nor are we attending to the screen on which they appear. This is obvious once we think of a case in which we *would* say we are looking at the images—when there is something *wrong* with the images, say, when they're blurred or grainy or oddly colored, and our job is to correct the problem. But in the normal case of watching a movie we don't focus our attention on those fleeting patterns of light—we, as it were, look right *through* them. What we look through them *to* I shall consider later; for now I hope it is clear that we are not, in the normal case, looking *at* the images that we indisputably see. They, after all, are not the point of the exercise; it is what they *depict* or *represent* that interests us, whatever precisely this may be. The images are merely vehicles to direct our attention elsewhere, so there is no point in scrutinizing them for their own sake. They fade into the background, so to speak. Vision does not relate to the screen by making us look at what is (literally) *on* the screen, as opposed to what it is that the image on the screen depicts. Watching a movie is therefore not a matter of attending to the images on the screen, even though seeing those images is essential to the enterprise. It is a little like listening to someone speaking: you don't normally attend to the words themselves, as acoustic signals, you attend to what the words *mean.*

So is there *no* kind of looking that relates us to the images on the screen? I earlier used the phrase "look through" and noted that what we look through we don't look at (say, a window). We also speak of "looking *into*," as when we say that someone was looking into a pool of water (at something in the water). And it is certainly tempting to employ these concepts of looking through and looking into in application to the screen image: we look *into* the screen, *through* the images displayed upon it, and *at* whatever those images represent. Here is an interesting passage from the noted editor and sound designer Walter Murch: "With a theatrical film, particularly one in which the audience is fully engaged, the screen is not a surface, it is a magic window, sort of a looking glass through which your whole body passes and becomes engaged *in* the action *with* the characters on the screen. If you really like a film, you're not aware that you are sitting in a cinema watching a movie. Your responses are very different than they would be with television. Television is a 'look-at' medium, while cinema is a 'look-into' medium."[1] I think that Murch is onto a good point here, and I want to elaborate on the point in a way he does not. As a visual art, cinema invites the response of looking *into* the medium, as opposed to *at* it—and hence (though Murch does not explicitly say this) *through* the medium toward something else. We look into and through the very thing that we see—the image on the screen. The screen functions like a window onto a world beyond, through which the eye naturally and spontaneously passes. (I'm not sure about "your whole body" passing through.) There is a kind of *transparency* to the cinematic image, in the sense that it is a medium that effaces itself in the act of looking: it doesn't seek your attention, but is content to direct it elsewhere. It is almost as if it gets embarrassed if it becomes an object of attentive looking, as when it appears blurry or fragmented or otherwise conspicuous; it prefers to occupy the background, not be thrust into the spotlight. It says: "See me, by all means; but please don't *look* at me."

This insight suggests a promising line of inquiry: what *other* things, in nature or human culture, are looked into rather than at? If there are such things, they will bear a significant analogy to movies, at least so far as our perceptual relation to them is concerned, and may even function as the perceptual prototype of movie watching. It should be noted first, however, that the other senses do not seem to attract the same kind of concept—we don't speak of touching into or smelling into or tasting into or even hearing into. I can listen *to* something, as opposed to merely hearing it, but there is no sense in the idea of listening *into* something—there is no auditory analogue of the idea of a *transparent* medium through which something else may be glimpsed or examined. The distinction between "into" and "at" applies only to the visual case. Accordingly, there is no other art form that exploits this type of distinction—no kind of music, say, that involves hearing *into* one sound in order to attend *to* another.

So, what else do we look into, and how do these things compare to movie screens? Here is a list, as exhaustive as I can make it: holes, water, windows, mirrors, microscopes, telescopes, the sky, flames, eyes, and the mind. I'll say something about each of these in turn.

THINGS TO LOOK INTO

Holes or cavities are perhaps the basic case of things you can look into: you can look into a well, say, possibly in search of something else, and you can look into a room to see if a certain person is in there. In a sense, the whole universe can be regarded as a combination of objects and holes—things in space. You can look into space, which is really just a giant hole into which everything fits (though it is not a hole *in* anything). A hole is a kind of visible (but intangible) nothingness—an absence of objects. A hole has no texture, though it has contours; and while you *can* look *at* a hole (as you can look at a movie image), you typically look through it to what it contains. Holes are modest creatures, content to house other entities, to which they graciously direct the inquiring eye; they don't want to be visually lingered over. In this they resemble the movie screen, which also plays host to other entities, to which it self-effacingly directs the attention of the viewer. The orifices of the body—holes in flesh—may also be looked into (though it is not considered polite to do so in normal circumstances), the eye being the most interesting example, which I will shortly consider in its own right. Whenever anything can be looked into, it is fair to say that it resembles a regular hole in some way—there is something holelike about it. The movie screen is aptly described as a *portal,* which is itself a hole of a certain sort (of the doorlike kind)—a hole for viewing things through. Describing the screen as a window also aligns it with a certain type of hole—the kind that appears in walls.

Water can be looked into, though it lacks the extreme nothingness of holes, but only when it is transparent or translucent—muddy water won't do. Think of being in an aquarium and gazing at the fish on display: you look *into* the water *for* the fish, but not *into* the fish. Or consider looking at coins at the bottom of a clear fountain: the eye leapfrogs over the liquid medium and is seized by the objects within. But it is not that the water is invisible; you see it, though it is not something at which the eye stops, at which it ceases to search. Water cries out to be looked through, used as a visual conduit. Nor do its shimmers and eddies inhibit the process; they may even add to the fascination of what is gazed upon. Similarly, the movie screen shimmers and writhes, being alive with movement and reflected light; yet, despite this activity, it is still more a medium of vision than an object of vision. The endless visual fascination of water in motion is mirrored in the fascination of the screen, which indeed can present an oceanic aspect. Water *on* the screen therefore comports naturally with the water *of* the screen: it is as if we are seeing water in water. Underwater photography is a graphic reminder of what the screen is doing anyway—enabling us to look through it as if it were a transparent liquid. Looking through water depicted on the screen enhances the looking through that is going on when we see the screen itself—it gets the eye in the mood, so to speak, for the looking-through experience. You find yourself looking through seawater at a looming shark, say, and this aids the looking through that the screen itself invites.

Sometimes we don't see windows, in which case there is a danger of inadvertently stepping through them, but mostly we do see them, because of grime and glinting. Yet we don't much care to scrutinize them; we are far more interested in what lies on their other side. We gaze out through a window at the world beyond or we gaze into a window at the room that it encloses. A window is an interface between the domestic or human world and the world of nature, since windows typically occur in *buildings*. It is really quite amazing how much people like to look into shop windows—far more than they do at the goods that lie on their other side. The eye is irresistibly drawn to windows, either for the outside view or for the inside view—the world of danger and the world of safety, we might say. A room without a window is a dismal place. But, as it is often remarked, the movie screen is a windowlike structure: it appears as a large bright window on a dark wall, and through it we can be the spectators of an entire new world. Yet it is a one-way window, since no one on the other side can see us as we drink them in with our eyes (this connects with the voyeurism of film watching, which I will also come back to). The curtain across the screen is like a curtain over a window, and a projector is simply a device for letting in the light (though, of course, it is really the source of the light). The movie screen is like a window onto a whole world, too, not just a particular segment of the neighborhood, for the camera is infinitely flexible in what it can present through this magic window. Being windowlike, the screen pulls the eye in, sending it in search of objects of interest.

Mirrors also are scarcely ever looked at—their entire purpose is to reflect objects other than themselves. We look into the mirror and beyond it, at our face and body, as if the mirror weren't there (though we know it is). Mirrors may serve our vanity; they have none of their own. It is virtually impossible to look *at* a mirror, unless it has defects; the eye bounces off the surface toward what it so slavishly reflects. A mirror provides a literal re-creation of something else—it is a device for doubling. It takes reality and re-presents it, gives it another chance at being, reincarnates it. A mirror is simply another way for the eye to see reality, enjoying only a vanishing existence of its own. Mirrors hide behind their own reflective power. And, of course, much the same can be said of the movie screen: it reflects what was earlier before the camera, a vision of reality, rather than intruding upon our visual consciousness itself. I *see* the movie screen, as I see the mirror I am looking into, but I look *at* the reality reflected or represented in it. Of course, it is a kind of delayed-action mirror, since the events reflected are not occurring at the time of the viewing; nevertheless, the screen works to convey to us a reality other than itself. The eye is working in much the same way when it takes in the movie image as it is when gazing at a reflection, in that it engages in an act of looking into—bouncing off a surface in the direction of what the surface portrays.

Microscopes and telescopes have more of a technical than a metaphorical relation to the screen. You look into the lens of the apparatus (transparent glass, like the window) and gaze upon the enlarged object of sight. The lens magnifies what comes within its scope, giving us a close-up of the object. The lens is not normally looked at or attended to; it is merely the means by which an object comes under our scrutiny with altered dimensions. This enlarging effect is, of course, a mainstay of the movie screen: the greatly magnified figures, the facial close-up, the new proximity of eye and object. By looking through an enlarging optical apparatus we are treated to a different visual perspective on the world, in which the natural limitations of the human eye are transcended, offering us a newly intimate relationship to nature. There is something startling about this perspective, sometimes disturbing, as normal-sized objects are rendered gargantuan. What we are looking at, by looking into the apparatus before us, is the world as it might be seen by another type of being, with more acute vision than ours. And this is a kind of magical effect, as if conferring a godlike power on our perception of reality. Not only does the screen let us look through it to a world not our own; it presents that world in startlingly magnified dimensions and detail, adopting the position of microscope. And we don't have to move at all: the enlarged world is brought to us, at a safe and convenient distance. When we see the world on a movie screen, it is as if we are seeing it with microscopes attached to our eyes. Thus *we* are magnified, enhanced, along with reality.

The sky is as old a friend to humankind as the earth itself: when did humans not gaze up into the sky? Day and night, the sky is one of the most entrancing of visual objects. Over millions of years our eyes have evolved with the sky as their primordial companion, always hanging there, waiting to be seen. Surely, the human eye is as adapted to the sky as it is adapted to anything, limited as its viewpoint is. Clouds, stars, and birds are among the objects the sky offers our visual system. We look up into the sky and look at these objects, laid out before us in an infinitely expansive medium, bounded only by the line of the earth's surface. Think of the absolutely trillions of times a human being has looked into the sky and noticed the objects within it, and reflect on what the eye has become because of these innumerable visual acts. Well, it is that eye that now finds itself confronted by a rather recent invention, the movie screen. And just as it has looked into the sky over eons of time, now it is called upon to look into the movie screen.

We can note two things about this development. First, the eye is doing now what it has been doing, and doing expertly, for millennia—it is *good* at this looking-into business. The sky has taught the human eye how to look into things, and the movie screen is just a fresh turn on an ancient skill. Looking into the screen is therefore *natural* to us, despite the recency of the technology. Secondly, whatever aura of mystery or fascination attaches to the sky—and surely a lot does—will transfer itself by analogy to the screen: it too will strike us as an entity of mythic proportions, as a repository of wonders. The sky always reminds me of our tiny place in the universe, the vastness in which we shudder and strive, both friendly and hostile, acutely unending. If the movie screen inherits even some small percentage of this awe, it will be invested with a significance it would be hard to overestimate. And the looking into that it invites must surely resonate with the looking into that the sky so primordially evokes. It is not surprising, from this perspective, that films so often open with a shot of the sky, since this introduces from the outset the basic mechanism of looking into, which is critical to the success of the film: the viewer's attention must be taken off the screen and onto what it transmits. And what is more visually gripping than the sight of an object flashing across the sky? The screen is tapping into these ancient and deep-seated aspects of our visual human nature, exploiting them for its own purposes.

As an extra piece of evidence for this analogy between sky and screen, consider what may not be a coincidence of nomenclature—the use of the word "star" in both connections. There are the stars of the blackened night sky, arrayed and twinkling, aloof, distant, not shrinking from our awe-struck gaze—the celebrities of the heavens; and there are those effects of light in human form, flitting across the capacious screen, remote yet intimate, shining, perfect—the film stars that equally populate our imagination. I venture to suggest that the use of the word "star" in application to film actors derives from its use to name the denizens of the night sky, and *not* vice versa. Then whoever it was who first employed that astronomical term in application to human beings must have been thinking of the stars of the sky, and hence analogizing sky and screen. As we wait for Venus to make its nightly appearance, bright and reassuring, changeless, so we wait for our favorite film star to wander into camera range and so fulfill our desire to have him or her in close proximity, shining just for us. And what is the role of the mighty sun in all this? Why, the all-powerful Director in the Sky, author of numberless epic sequels, repelling our curious gaze—he around whom everything revolves. The ancient Greeks identified the stars with the gods, not preposterously given their limited cosmological knowledge; now we make that identification for the heavenly bodies of Hollywood (among other notables). The sky is where we expect divinity to reside, and the screen is the sky rendered manageable. If we could project movies onto the massive dome of the sky, I don't doubt we would find it more satisfying (if somewhat uneconomical) to watch them that way. In any case, the eye's capacity to look into the movie screen has its precedent in our visual relation to the sky.

Fire has not been with the human race for as long as the sky, but it has had a pretty long run. And gazing into flames is no doubt an ancient pastime (usurped somewhat by television). We can see strange and fascinating patterns there, projections of our own fears and longings, as we bask in the congenial warmth. Flames are a medium we can look into, in hopes perhaps of finding something else (the meaning of life, whether the crops will survive). Here is Walter Murch on flames and films:

> The mid-twentieth-century pessimism about the future of cinema, which foresaw a future ruled by television, overlooked the perennial human urge—at least as old as language itself—to leave the home and assemble in the fire-lit

> dark with like-minded strangers to listen to stories. The cinematic experience is a recreation of this ancient practice of theatrical renewal and bonding in modern terms, except the flames of the stone-age campfire have been replaced by the shifting images that are telling the story itself. Images that dance the same way every time the film is projected, but which kindle different dreams in the mind of each beholder.[2]

I am not sure that there is really a contrast with television here—the fire just seems smaller on the TV than on the movie screen—but I would agree that there is a similarity between gazing into the flames while one's imagination runs riot and gazing into the screen, where also the imagination is actively recruited. Both consist of flickering light—volatile, mobile, and suggestive—and both seem to refer the mind to things beyond themselves. "Look into me," both seem to say, "and I will show you marvelous things." Is it any surprise, then, that fire should be such a recurrent motif (or gimmick) of motion pictures? We are simply seeing on the screen what the screen itself mimics. And is it too much to suggest that the movie screen might also mimic some of the comfort and security provided by the warm and pleasant fire, as well as containing a hint of danger? Certainly, there is a gap left by the retreat of the open communal fire from human life, and maybe cinema steps in to fill it (as well as doing many other things). I myself have a great fondness for open fires, the bigger the better, and I am also quite fond of movies.

I have so far spoken of the eye as it engages with the screen, but there is also the matter of the eye *on* the screen—and the relation of the looking-into concept to the seen eye (as opposed to the seeing eye). For we certainly do speak of looking *into* a person's eyes, despite the relative solidity and opacity of the anatomical organs in question. True, eyes are glassy and aqueous, like windows and water, but they are also round and nuggetlike, a far cry from sky or fire. Looking *at* a person's eyes is very different from looking *into* them, and the former is done usually only by ocular professionals. When I look into your eyes, what is it that I am looking at? You, of course—I am looking at you. And I am looking at a very significant part of you—the part often designated "the soul," the eyes being commonly said to be the window to that entity. I am seeing your *self.* So I am looking at something other than your body—I am looking at something psychological in nature, the "I." No such sighting of the self is possible if I look into your nose or ears—just very unsoul-like grunge. Only the organs we call the eyes seem to afford us a glimpse of the self. When the lover gazes into the eyes of his beloved, he is greeted not merely by a pair of glistening orbs but by the very pith of the person he loves—so, at least, we suppose; that's what it *feels* like. The eye is, as it were, an inlet through which the self within can escape the opacity of the human body—the point of maximal psychological openness. Securing or avoiding "eye contact" is all about this exposure of the self through the eyes. As social beings, needing to read each other's psychology, we are adept at this kind of looking into—at reading the mind off the eye. In the geography of the human body, the mind sails closest to the eye, and we are gifted observers of this phantom vessel. Looking into the sky and looking into the eye must be our most basic exercises of the capacity to look into things.

The very capacity we use to interpret the screen we use to interpret a person's eyes. Thus the screen resembles the eye. The reflective twinkling eye finds its analogue in the reflecting surface of the lit screen—predominantly because both are not objects to be looked *at,* but *into* and *through.* And what do we become aware of as we look into the screen? The *persons* depicted, of course—those psychologically charged beings. As I look into the screen, I become aware of the motivations, beliefs, and personalities of the individuals depicted, just as I become aware of these things when I look into a person's eyes. I look through the screen to the souls, so to speak, with the screen a mere vehicle, a means to an end. Also, as before, it is not merely that the screen itself resembles the eye; the eye is also one of the great subjects *of* the screen. Indeed, I would go so far as to suggest that it is *the* great subject of cinema. The act of looking into is common to both screen and eye, and hence the appearance of the eye on the screen invites the very capacity called upon by the screen itself—what we might call the "look-into reflex." Once the camera homes in on the eye, suitably lit and positioned, we are ineluctably drawn in through the barrier of the screen—we are in "look-into mode." The screened eye commits us to an act of *double* looking into: first into the screen itself and then into the eye on the screen (equivalently, into the image of the eye and then into the eye imaged). By this time the screen has dissolved before us, fading into its role as vehicle. The screen has no call on our attention, and only the rude jolt of imperfection in the image can snap our attention back from the depicted world—a most undesirable rebound. The screened eye is perhaps the most reliable way for a film to bind us to the looking-into mode of visual reception. The viewer's eye becomes entranced by the eye on the screen, into which it looks, and the pattern of images disappears—seen but not attended to. This use of the depicted eye is one of the most powerful tools of film in evoking the ancient reflex of looking into, upon which the effectiveness of cinema depends. It is the eye on the screen that most powerfully annihilates the screen for the viewer, to put it dramatically.

Finally, there is the mind as something to be looked into. I don't mean to suggest that we can literally peer into each other's minds—that is the sort of thing that believers in telepathy and the like subscribe to. But we do naturally conceive the mind in a way that makes it the *sort* of thing that could in principle be looked into. We seem comfortable with the notion of looking into one's *own* mind, as when we say: "I looked into myself and didn't like what I saw there." And it is also common to describe God's access to human minds in this way—he can see right into them, right through them, so that no secrets can be kept from his prying gaze. I know your mind by inference from your body—by how you behave—but God's vision can see straight into your soul, so that for God the mind is something that submits to being looked into. When God, as we say, looks into our mind, he is able to look *at* what it contains—those petty motives or self-serving beliefs. So the mind is being conceived as a kind of medium (like water, to which it is commonly compared—the "stream of consciousness" and all that) in which items of interest can be discerned and scrutinized, if the viewer has eyes of the right penetrative power. The body, by contrast, cannot be looked into, being substantial, solid, and opaque (I am not speaking of the orifices here). No doubt this is all very metaphorical, but it does correspond to something in our conception of what the mind or soul is—a containing medium. If so, there is an analogy between the mind and the screen, so that when we look into the screen it is (metaphorically) *as if* we are looking into a mind.

Because of this commonality, we might say that the mind is part of the *connotation* of the screen—what it suggests, the associations it has (no doubt implicitly); and similarly for the other entities I have cited as displaying the look-into property. Once again, this is reinforced by the fact that part of what the screen *displays* is mental in nature—that is, the psychological states of the characters depicted. We are confronted by minds on the screen (I shall defend this fully in the next chapter), and the screen itself works in a way analogous to the mind, in that it is the kind of thing that we tend to conceive in terms of the notion of looking into. And, of course, the eye of the actor directs us toward the mind of the character portrayed, so that the screen in effect offers us *three* things that can be looked into: itself, the eye, and the mind. The looking-at part of the total visual experience starts to seem, if not marginal, then not at any rate the distinctive crux of what watching a movie is. Movie watching is all about acts of looking into, one piled on top of another.

It might be objected to all this that the screen cannot be looked into in the same way other things can be, because it is a flat, two-dimensional surface—how can we look *into* something that has no depth or thickness? That would be like looking into a page or a tabletop. To be looked into, an entity needs to have depth, as holes, water, sky, fire, and eyes have depth. I take it the answer to this objection is obvious (and the case of mirrors might already have suggested it): the screen does not literally have the third dimension, but in a *representational* way it does. Depth is coded into what we see, apparent from the properties of the two-dimensional images on the flat screen (one object looks farther away than another when it corresponds to the smaller of the two images). Thus the eye is able to move through this virtual third dimension, to encounter the three-dimensional objects depicted on the flat screen. It is indeed doubtful that without this impression of depth the image on the screen could elicit the look-into reflex; but with it the screen is able to conduct the eye beyond itself. This is just to say that the cinema succeeds in creating a semblance of a real three-dimensional world—our ordinary space is very much present in the image. Rather like the flatness of mirrors, the flatness of the screen is therefore no impediment to its being looked into.

OTHER ARTS

Do any other visual art forms involve the type of looking I am calling looking into? Answering this question will enable us to determine whether this type of looking is *distinctive* of film. The arts we need to consider are theatre, painting, photography, television, sculpture, and architecture.

Theatre, quite clearly, requires no looking into, except in relation to the actors' eyes; but the medium itself—actors on a stage—no more calls for looking into than ordinary people in a room do. Of course, there is the space of the stage, but the objects before the eyes—props and human bodies—are not in any way transparent entities that we look *through*. The audience looks *at* these things, not through them; there is no analogue of the screen as a traversable medium standing between the eyes and objects. So the visual relation we have to the staged play is of a very different nature from that which obtains between the viewer and the cinema screen; the visual system is differently engaged in the two cases, despite the fact that both at some point involve actors moving through space. The eye is not drawn through the events on the stage as it is through the images on the screen; the eye reacts differently to the actors on the stage and the images on the screen, though both are what are immediately *seen*. In short, we look at the stage actors but not at the movie images. We could say that visually speaking, theatre is a *present* medium while cinema is an *absent* medium. Cinema is self-effacing while theatre is self-affirming. The cinema screen is there to be transcended; the stage is the primary object of attention. The screen confronts you with something it wants you to ignore; the stage wants to hold your attention on itself.

Painting presents a subtler issue. It is two-dimensional, like cinema, and it presents the viewer with an image of an absent object, also like cinema. Unlike the stage, painting is a *representation* of people and things, not real people and real things. But do we look *into* a painting (as opposed to the eyes in a portrait)? I think not: we look *at* a painting. We stand before the painting and admire *it*—we scrutinize it, let our eyes linger over the painted canvas. In no way does the painting become invisible to us—it is the object of our visual attention. The painting is not a visual route to something else; it is the perceptual end point of the process. So the canvas is not, from a visual point of view, like a movie screen. And, of course, the two are differently constituted: the painting consists of pigments on a flat surface, which themselves reflect the light; the movie image consists of projected light on a flat surface, which does not itself reflect light. One is a chemical phenomenon; the other is a phenomenon of pure light. The two types of image are made of completely different physical materials, and this is evident to the eye of the viewer. Incident light enhances the painterly image, but it destroys the movie image, since it competes with the light on the screen (this is why movie theatres are dark and art galleries light). The way light reflects from the surface of a painting gives the painting a *texture,* which is evident to the viewer's eye—we know that it will feel a certain way if touched (bumpy, smooth in places). The painting is perceived to be a *surface,* just like the surface of a table or a carpet, and its properties are manifest in the way it reflects light. But none of this is true of the movie image: *it has no texture.* It is not that incident light reflects the antecedent condition of the screen (nothing is imprinted on it before the projector starts); rather, the projected light is itself the image. This image tells us nothing *about the screen:* the light of the movie image does not reveal what the surface of the screen is really like, as the light falling on a painting reveals its standing surface features. Accordingly, we do not admire and scrutinize the screen as a surface, but proceed visually to another plane. We look into and beyond this textureless mirage; but in the case of painting we are confronted, as it were, with a flesh-and-blood object—a solid material thing, opaque and reflective in its own right. Moving paintings, if such there could be, would not engage the eye in the same way that the light-constituted movie image does—they would still be objects of, and for, the attention. This is why we marvel at, say, the way Turner uses paint to represent light, but we don't lavish the same praise and attention on the way the light on a movie screen represents light. The medium of painting—pigments on canvas—is not an *absent* medium, perceptually speaking. So the way we look at a painting is *not* analogous to the way we visually apprehend holes, water, the sky, the eyes, and so on; and so it stands in contrast to our visual relation to the screen.

The case of photography might seem to fall on the side of the movie image, since movie images precisely are photographic images. If we look through or into cinematic photographs, must we not also look through or into the kind of photographs that are imprinted on pieces of paper? However, a regular photograph is a chemical effect imprinted onto paper: it reflects light, it has a texture, and it appears as a surface. Thus we naturally invite each other to look *at* photographs ("Look at this picture of me in Cancun," etc.).

Of course, as with paintings, we also see this looked-at object as *representing* something, a person, say; but we do not thereby look *into* the photograph. We look at the photograph and see it as representing something, but we don't look at the movie image and thereby see it as representing something. The movie image is seen but not looked at; the photograph is seen *and* looked at (and not just when it is defective). The reason for the difference is not that one is moving and the other is not; it is that one is seen as a textured surface and the other is not. This is why looking at a photograph of X is not like seeing X through a pool of clear water, though seeing X in a screen image is. Photographs are objects of visual attention; movies exist to direct attention elsewhere (soon I shall say where).

But surely, it may be said, television is just like movies, for don't we watch movies on television? When the eye is fixated on the television screen, and the viewer is immersed in the action of the movie he or she is watching, isn't there equally an act of looking into? Isn't the television screen just as self-effacing as the movie screen? And yet, don't we prefer to see a movie at a movie theatre? (We stay home for practical, not aesthetic, reasons.) Somehow, we feel, it *works* better there, no matter how wide and flat our TV screen may be. The question is whether this shows that TV screens are not the kind of thing we look *into.*

Now it is not that we can never in principle look into a movie-screen image in our own home (some people have private movie theatres, after all); but I do think there remains a significant point of difference between the two types of screen, arising simply from the physical nature of the TV screen. For the TV screen itself—a piece of rectangular glass sitting in front of the viewer—is an object that can all too easily become a visual surface in its own right, as when light from the window or a lamp falls across its glassy face. Then we find our attention distracted from the film we are watching to the medium of our watching it; the screen asserts its identity, its solidity, its thingness. Dust on the screen, combined with incident light, will inhibit the looking into that the screened film yearns to generate. We can never quite make the TV screen go away. We are always looking at a bulky piece of hardware that is on the brink of gaining our attention. The TV set is uncomfortably close to being a piece of *furniture*—not an impalpable magic window onto another world. The kind of immersion characteristic of the cinema experience never quite occurs in the domestic embrace of the TV screen. We never quite enter the world of the film that is being broadcast as we do in the movie theatre. The typical television set is just too *small* to escape its identity as one object in the visual field among many—as just one of the things competing for our attention. By contrast, because of its sheer size, the movie screen can hardly be singled out within the visual field as one object among many; hence its capacity to assume the dimensions of a whole world. This is why we naturally say that we look at our television screens, but we don't find ourselves saying this about the movie screen. The TV apparatus is *intrusive* in a way that the movie apparatus is not.

Sculpture and architecture require little comment, though I think both can in a certain way quite easily evoke the looking-into response. Suppose a sculpture (say, a Henry Moore) has *holes* in it—aren't these the paradigm of things that can be looked into? Now I don't want to take a stand on whether a hole in a statue is really *part* of the statue, but I take it this case does nothing to show that sculpture itself is of its very nature a look-into medium, since clearly the solid bits are what sculpture is all about, and they obviously resist any attempt at looking into. Sculpture is all solidity and texture, and it cries out to be looked at (the only kind of sculpture you could look through would be made of transparent materials). Architecture, another three-dimensional visual art, can also invite looking into, as when you enter a cathedral and look into the space within, or look into a room through a window. But, again, this is a contingent aspect of it, drawing upon other looked-into media; it is not constitutive of architectural objects that their appreciation involves sustained and systematic looking into. Certainly, gazing at a building from the outside is a clear case of looking *at;* the building does not work to conduct your visual attention elsewhere. The stone façade of a building is nothing like a movie screen, so far as perception is concerned.

I conclude, then, that *only* cinema, among the visual arts, constitutively requires looking into as part of its proper appreciation. (I have not denied that it is *possible* to look at the movie image itself, even when it is flawless; but this is not the typical stance and detracts from the power of the film.) This isn't to say that there *could* not be an art form that also required such looking into—say, a type of artwork that involved placing objects in a watery medium—but as things stand, cinema is distinguished by this perceptual phenomenon. A person who lacked the look-into ability could not fully enter into the movie experience, since he could not take his attention off the screen itself and its play of light images. But we normal humans are amply gifted with this capacity. Thanks to our experience with holes, the sky, the eyes, and so on, looking into things comes naturally to us.

WHAT ARE WE LOOKING AT?

What is it that we *do* look at when we are watching a movie? Let us consider a particular case—say, watching *Citizen Kane.* There is the image on the screen, a particular pattern of light; there is the actor Orson Welles, very much more substantial than a slice of light; and there is the character of Charles Foster Kane, who is by no means to be identified with Welles himself. We are not looking at the first element in this triad (though we are seeing it); so which of the other two is the object of our looking? Actually, we need to add a third possibility: nothing, no one—perhaps we are looking at nothing whatsoever, there is no object of our looking here. Not to keep the reader in suspense, I think that we are looking at Orson Welles, not at nothing and not at the fictional character he plays. We look through the image of Welles to the man himself—*he* is the thing we are looking at, that flesh-and-blood actor. It can't be that we are looking at nothing, since if we are looking into one thing we must thereby be looking at another. There is no *pure* looking into; all acts of looking into are accompanied by acts of looking at. And if there is an act of looking at, then there has to be an *object* of looking at. Nor, I think, is Charles Foster Kane the thing we are looking at, for we are not *seeing* him. It is not Kane who stands before the camera, causing the image that confronts us on the screen; it is Welles. Kane is an *imaginary* character. Our relation to Kane is mediated by our imagination, not the mere act of seeing. We *see* the image of Welles and we *imagine* Kane. You could, in principle, see the image of Welles and *not* imagine Kane, if you had no idea that this is a fictional work about an errant newspaper tycoon. The thing we are looking at, then, is the thing we are seeing; and this is Welles, not Kane. We don't need to imagine Welles in order for him to be an object of our acquaintance, since he is present to our mind by means of the photographic process: there is a causal chain leading from him to our visual experience in the cinema. But there is no such chain from Kane to our visual experience, because Kane was not being photographed when the film was made; only Welles was. You can't photograph fictional characters, only the real people who play them. Nor can fictional characters be literally looked at.

So, the right description of this complex visual relationship is as follows: the image on the screen is seen but not looked at; the actor is seen and looked at; the fictional character is neither seen nor looked at, but imagined. Different actors can play the same character, and when this happens many individuals will be looked at by the audience, not the single character they all play—though it is a single character that is imagined by all. By the same reasoning, if a movie uses a prop to stand in for a real object—say, a model city—then the thing the audience is looking at and seeing is the actual prop model, not the full-size city they imagine in connection with it. This has the consequence that audiences don't always know what they are looking at; they can make mistakes about this—they think it's a real city when it is just a model. What you are looking at and seeing is what was before the camera at the time of shooting, and you may have completely wrong ideas about what that object was.

RECIPROCAL SEEING

What is the precise relationship between the image seen and the actor (or object) seen? You see both when you watch a movie, but these are not unrelated acts of seeing; they are intimately connected. A notion often introduced in connection with pictorial perception is Ludwig Wittgenstein's notion of *seeing as*.[3] The idea is that you see the image *as* Welles or as a man of such-and-such physical appearance. You don't just see the image as a patch of light; you see it as representative of a three-dimensional human being. Alternatively, we could say that you see Welles—the man—*in* the image on the screen. You invest the image with this real-life reference, so that the seeing has two aspects: what it is a seeing *of* (the image) and what it is a seeing *as* (a man). Thus the seeing has a kind of inner complexity, bringing two objects into close relation: the image and what it is an image of. It isn't just that you see the image *and* you see the object it represents; you see the object by *means* of the image.

This seems to me a perfectly adequate way to capture the nature of the cinematic visual experience, but I want to add something to it, to enrich it in a certain way. To do this, I shall introduce the notion of *reciprocal seeing.* The point of this notion is that the seeing of the one thing essentially involves the seeing of the other—each seeing leads into the other one. The seeings are joined at the hip, as it were. When you see the image (in normal circumstances), you also and thereby see the object—you see Welles by seeing an image of him. Indeed, seeing the image enables you to see through *to* Welles. But it is equally true that your seeing Welles this way involves your seeing him *under the aspect* of an image. It is not that you see Welles just as you would if he were standing before you, unmediated by any image of him; rather, your seeing of him comes in another mode—that of image-mediated seeing. You see the image as Welles, but you also see Welles as presented by an image. The image leads you to the object, but the object leads you back to the image—hence *reciprocal* seeing. In Wittgenstein's famous example of the duck/rabbit drawing, you see the drawing as a duck, say, but in seeing this duck you see it *as represented by an ambiguous drawing.* That's the way the duck comes to you perceptually, and it is very different from the ordinary seeing of ducks. Each episode of seeing embeds the other. Similarly, in seeing the movie image, your seeing of the image embeds a seeing of the represented object, but your seeing of the object also embeds a seeing of the image. When you see Welles by means of his image, he comes to you very differently from an ordinary seeing of him, which is why you don't take yourself to have Welles in the theatre with you. We have indissoluble double seeing here, each seeing conditioned or modified by the other. And as I have said, one of these events of seeing is accompanied by an act of looking through while the other is accompanied by an act of looking at. It is not that each seeing is a *barrier* to the other, as if they were in competition for our visual resources; on the contrary, each seeing points toward the other. Abstractly put, I see X as Y *and* I see Y as X.

The image represents an object; the object does not represent an image (Welles the man is not a *symbol* standing for his image). So the representation relation is not symmetrical: it is not in general true that if X represents Y, Y represents X (my name represents or refers to me, but I do not represent or refer to my name). Now some kinds of representation stand for their objects in an entirely extrinsic way—it is not possible to perceive their reference just by perceiving them. Thus words have reference, but they do so extrinsically, since you can see or hear a word and not see or hear the thing it stands for. This is basically because a word is a *conventional* symbol: the connection between word and object is arbitrary, not natural. The reference of a proper name, like "Horatio Alger," is clearly not embedded *in* the name (considered as a mark or sound); you cannot gain perceptual access to the reference, a certain man, just by perceiving the name. But in the case of movie images (and maybe photographs in general) we do have embedded reference: by seeing the representation we do gain perceptual access to the reference—we see Welles just by seeing his image on the screen (though seeing his *name* on the screen gives no such access). This is because photographic images are *not* merely conventional or arbitrary. Notice that I am defining "embedded reference" in perceptual terms: we can *see* the reference of a movie image by seeing the image; I am not saying that the object is *physically* embedded in the image, as a piece of food might be embedded between my teeth. Welles the man is very distant from his image when I see him in it—he isn't somehow stuck inside the image, like a caged animal. But it is still true that I am made able to see him by means of the presence of his image.

The notion of embedded reference enables us to recognize a significant feature of the movie-watching experience: that we are perceptually connected to objects in the real world and not merely to arbitrary symbols that flash before our eyes. It is emphatically *not* like hearing a language to which you must *attach* reference: it is not that you first see the images and then have to go about interpreting them according to some conventional scheme. It is rather that the object *comes with* the image: in seeing the one I thereby see the other. Picture recognition works very differently from word recognition. Once a child has learned how to recognize objects—to classify them in appropriate ways—she has nothing more to learn in recognizing pictures of objects: if she can recognize an object as an apple, she can also recognize something as a picture of an apple (once she has got the general hang of pictorial representation). The converse is also true: once you can recognize pictures of things, there is nothing further you need to master in order to recognize the things that are pictured—which is why a photograph can be decisive in tracking down a fugitive. But nothing like this holds for language or any other conventional symbolic system: you can be excellent at recognizing apples but have no ability to recognize that some sound you hear *means* apples. If you could make this step, learning foreign languages would be a piece of cake! For that, you need to learn the language as an independent entity—a skill that goes far beyond the recognition of objects themselves. The relation between pictures and things is very different from the relation between words and things. Given the notion of embedded reference, this is just what we would expect, since the image embeds the object, so that the very same skill we use for recognizing the object will be employed in recognizing the picture of the object. By contrast, when the reference is not embedded, but extrinsic, as with words, we cannot use the object-recognition skill in their interpretation. Put simply, I can see you in a photograph of you, but I cannot see you just by looking at your name.

Let me now summarize these ideas. Watching a film involves the reciprocal seeing of images and objects, where the object is an embedded referent of the image. In seeing the image we look through it to the object embedded in it, which we look at (the actor, not the character). The image is transparent in the sense that it permits looking into; the object is not transparent in this sense. The fictional characters portrayed are imagined on the basis of all this seeing and looking, but they are not themselves seen or looked at. When we watch a movie, there is a lot going on perceptually, despite the ease with which we do it.

REALISM AND FORMALISM

This analysis has a direct bearing on one of the classic questions of film theory—realism vs. formalism. Early enthusiasts of cinema, such as Hugo Munsterberg and Rudolf Arnheim, were anxious to demonstrate its distance from theatre and from the mere recording of nature, so that its status as an autonomous art form could be established.[4] They accordingly stressed the formal properties of film as essential to its aesthetic effect—the way that the medium of film itself imposed its own identity upon the images projected onto the screen. Film was not to be seen as the passive recording of reality—a mere rehashing of ordinary perception—but as a distinctive medium by which the filmmaker could express his artistic vision. Film was compared to music and to literature, which no one could accuse of merely replicating reality (as a waxwork does). The use of montage, in particular, was felt to free cinema from the constraints of reality, since it allowed the filmmaker to sequence his images in ways not sanctioned by nature, but as expressive of the filmmaker's imagination. This, in brief, is the formalist school, which stresses the contribution made by the film medium itself. The emphasis was all on the images themselves, not on what they are images *of.*

Rebelling against this retreat from the world, the realist school, represented by Siegfried Kracauer and André Bazin, insisted that the photographic nature of cinema rendered it uniquely revelatory of objective reality: film by its nature presents raw reality to us, and this is its defining strength as an art form.[5] Bazin writes: "In no sense is it [photography] the image of an object or person, more correctly it is its tracing. Its automatic genesis distinguishes it radically from other techniques of reproduction. The photograph proceeds by means of the lens to the taking of a veritable luminous impression in light—to a mold. As such it carries with it more than mere resemblance, namely a kind of identity—the card we call by that name being only conceivable in an age of photography."[6] Even more forthrightly, he asserts: "The photographic image is the object itself, the object freed from the conditions of time and space that govern it. No matter how fuzzy, distorted, or discolored, no matter how lacking in documentary value the image may be, it shares, by the very process of its becoming, the being of the model of which it is the reproduction; it *is* the model."[7] This is a strong statement indeed of the realist position, maintaining as it does that there is literally an *identity* between the image on the screen and the object it depicts. On this view, it is quite unapt to compare cinema to music or literature, since these art forms do not harbor any identity between themselves and what they are about: they represent things without *being* those things. By contrast, Bazin believes that movies, in virtue of their basis in photography, literally bring the world to the screen, so much so that it is wrong to describe what we see on the screen as an *image* at all. What we see at the movies is reality itself, period. The emphasis here is all on what the image is of and not what it is in itself.

Now both these theories stake out extreme positions; the truth lies somewhere between them. Film is not like a language that can be manipulated by the filmmaker to convey his imaginative products, with no essential relation to reality: it is not a *conventional* mode of representation, but a kind of automatic depiction effected by light and lenses. Film images are not like musical notes or words on the page. But neither is it correct to assert that the image on the screen *is* the object depicted, since one is a smudge of light and the other is a solid chunk of matter. Watching an actor on screen is not exactly like watching him on the stage. I suggest that the ideas of reciprocal seeing and embedded reference enable us to formulate the correct intermediate position. When you see the image, you thereby see the object; but the object is not seen except under the aspect of the image: form and content are inextricably combined here. It is not that your visual response is confined to one or the other of these entities—the image to the exclusion of the object or the object stripped of its mediation by the image. *You see both,* and this in such a way as to include one act of seeing in the other. By virtue of the mechanism of embedded reference you are able to apprehend the object simply by apprehending the image of it, but in no sense is it true that the embedded reference *is* the image in which it is embedded. It is just that photographic images can generate a perceptual relation to the object photographed, as mere words cannot. There is indeed a distinctive medium of film, as the formalists supposed, but it doesn't work to exclude the object from the film medium; and there is a special kind of connection to reality, as the realists insisted, but it is not that reality swallows up the medium. Perceptually, we relate both to the film medium *and* to the reality it presents, since the medium precisely is an invocation of reality—what stood before the camera lens and left its trace. So the notion of embedded reference and the theory of movie perception as reciprocal seeing allow us to extract the kernel of truth from both the extreme formalist and the extreme realist position. True, the image is a two-dimensional entity, not a three-dimensional one like the object depicted, so that there can be no identity between image and object; but it is misleading to suggest that the image cannot provide us with a way of perceiving the depicted object—it is just that this perception is mediated by the image. After all, the image projected onto the retina when we see an ordinary object is two-dimensional, but that doesn't prevent us from seeing three-dimensional objects by means of this image. (I shall have more to say about the ontological disparity between images and objects in the next chapter; for now I am simply noting that this disparity does not preclude the idea that images enable us to see objects.)

Formalism and realism are, in effect, theories about the nature of the cinematic look. The formalist thinks that the image interposes itself between the viewer and the world, so that it is the image that the viewer looks at—the real world hovering quite elsewhere. The realist thinks that we do not attend to the image but to the object it depicts—hence we look at the object. As I have argued, the realist is right about this, but it is a mistake to infer that the image enjoys *no* perceptual relation to the viewer—as if she were simply looking right at an ordinary object. The looking at that is directed to the object is conditioned by the image, controlled by the image, made possible by the image. The image is incontrovertibly *seen.* Once we understand that the cinematic look incorporates in its essence both the medium of film *and* the subject matter of film, there should be no temptation to opt for either formalism or realism. You look into the image *in order to* look at the object. The image does not block off the object, and the object does not consume the image. The dispute between realism and formalism is a spurious dilemma, spawned by not properly analyzing the nature of our visual relation to the screen.

THE PLEASURE OF LOOKING

Much of the discussion of this chapter has been rather theoretical and abstract, though necessarily so if we are to set ourselves on firm foundations. So let me conclude with three topics that bring us back to the sensuous roots of movie watching: the face, visual pleasure, and voyeurism.

Close-ups can be of many things—hands, keys, guns—but it is the face for which the close-up seems designed. Our visual relationship to the screen consists very largely of watching close-ups of the human face (it would be interesting to know what percentage of film time is occupied in this way). The reason for this is evident: the face is what most powerfully conveys the interior life of the character—his or her thoughts, feelings, motivations, and so on. So the type of audience perception that comes into play here is not merely the perception of material things but of *states of mind.* You look into the screen and you see the terror on the face of the heroine, the villain's gloating and glee, the hero's resolve—you become aware of the psychological happenings that are so vital a part of the story. The facial close-up is what primarily guides your perception of the actors' states of mind. Bela Balazs, the film theorist, writes: "Good close-ups radiate a tender human attitude in the contemplation of hidden things, a delicate solicitude, a gentle bending over the intimacies of life-in-the-miniature, a warm sensibility. Good close-ups are lyrical; it is the heart, not the eye, that has perceived them."[8] He also observes that the spatiality of the face "loses all reference to space when we see, not a figure of flesh and bone, but an expression, or in other words when we see emotions, moods, intentions and thoughts, things which though our eyes can see them, are not in space."[9] In the close-up "we can see to the bottom of the soul by means of such tiny movements of facial muscles which even the most observant partner would never perceive."[10]

The close-up affords a uniquely powerful window onto the mind of the character, more powerful than any encountered in the world of ordinary perception. No such resource is available to the stage actor, since he is too far away from the audience. The face on the screen becomes a means of psychological revelation to which the viewer's eye is attuned. The close-up exploits what psychologists call "mind reading": the minds of the characters become overwhelmingly present to us—more so than in real life. Part of our visual relationship to the screen is a kind of magnified reading of minds—soul seeing, as it were. As I noted earlier, looking into the eyes of the actors aids this process enormously; the close-up of the eye is the central means of this cinematic mind reading. Without the close-up movies would lack much of their psychological power, their peculiar dramatic punch. The expressive possibilities of a screen actor's face are surely his or her strongest asset. Viewing the screen is a dynamic interplay between two minds, the actor's and the audience's; and the way we see and interpret faces is a central part of this.

We derive pleasure from our visual encounters with the screen, and sometimes no doubt this reflects the presence of beautiful objects on the screen, people or things. But we also appear to derive pleasure from the screened image as such: our eyes are drawn to the screen and they linger there with obvious delight (a faint smile often accompanies such lingering). Why is the screen a source of visual pleasure? I think there are two connected answers. The first goes back to our discussion of looking into; the very act of looking through one thing to see another gives us pleasure, as if our eyes were performing a magical feat—traversing one domain of reality to reach another. Often such looking is accompanied by visual curiosity—we are looking *for* something, something of interest or moment. We look into the sky or a person's eyes in order to discern something there that interests us—a star, a self. So the visual pleasure of the screen inherits the pleasure of looking into generally.

Secondly, there is the pleasure of *imaginative seeing*. Consider looking from an airplane through a blue sky to an accumulation of clouds: the clouds might be seen *as* a celestial city, with billowing buildings housing feathery citizens. This kind of imaginative seeing enables us to connect the world of imagination and the world of perception. We like to look at things that allow or encourage this kind of imaginative exercise (of course, imagining itself is often pleasurable). There is fun to be had in seeing as; children like to play this game in their pretend play. Well, in the movie theatre we also give free rein to our imagination, as we bring it to bear on the images that flit and dart before us: we imagine the characters, their predicaments, their feelings. It is not that we just passively observe things; we actively construct an interpretation of what we are seeing. It is as if the movie itself really took place in our minds, with the images on the screen acting as mere stimuli. Movie watching is inherently an imaginative act. And it is a kind of imaginative seeing—seeing impregnated with imagining. Movie watching has all the appeal of this kind of seeing—the delights of constructing imaginary worlds from suggestive stimuli. Part of the visual pleasure of movies derives from this conjoining of perception and imagination, of the outer with the inner, of the deterministic world and the free self. This pleasure exists alongside whatever pleasure we derive from the particular things that the screen offers our senses—faces, costumes, scenery, etc. The pleasure of movies is partly the pleasure of integrating what we bring from the inside with what the world imposes on our senses.

Then there is the vexed matter of voyeurism. The essence of voyeurism is the unreciprocated look: I look at you but you do not see me looking at you. In normal life, voyeurism requires concealment on the part of the onlooker, and typically distance. But the camera changes all that: *it* can look for me, while I safely skulk in hiding for what it relays to my heavy-breathing consciousness. Now I don't wish here to enter into a discussion of the psychological and ethical nature of voyeurism—whether it involves asymmetries of power or simply extreme curiosity, how good or bad it may be—but I take it that cinema is a medium in which voyeurism, in some form or measure, is part of the bargain. The feminist film theorist Laura Mulvey writes: "The extreme contrast between the darkness in the auditorium (which also isolates the spectators from one another) and the brilliance of the shifting patterns of light and shade on the screen helps to promote the illusion of voyeuristic separation. Although the film is really being shown, is there to be seen, conditions of screening and narrative conventions give the spectator an illusion of looking in on a private world."[11] Alfred Hitchcock notoriously associated film with the voyeuristic impulse and incorporated it into some of his films (notably *Rear Window*). In the case of the theatre, the actors have the power to stare right back at the audience—the audience is present to them. But film actors are deprived of this power; the audience is never within their field of gaze. The viewer is a voyeur almost by definition—even before we get to the question of sex scenes.

Three factors feed the voyeuristic appetite in the cinema: the close-up, looking into, and psychological foregrounding. In the close-up we can be voyeurs at extremely close quarters: not from one window into another across a dark street, but inches away from the observed individual. This is especially true of the face, whose detail is not revealed except at close quarters: you can see each telltale twitch of the actor's face, while yours is completely invisible to him or her. You can secretly sneer while the actor weeps, or cheer when the character dies, but you emerge unscathed from this act of intimate revelation. Returned eye contact is not a peril of these dramatic proceedings. Blatant staring carries no penalty in the form of a reproving glance. You can look right into the eye of the actor and your own eye has no reality for the object of your brazen gaze. The close-up gives the viewer as much covert access as he could possibly want (and pornography does not stint in respect of the fixated close-up).

Real-life voyeurism often involves peering unobserved into someone else's private space—normally, a room. It may also involve the use of an optical device, such as binoculars. It may take place through a window. All of these instigate feats of looking into, in search of the object to be looked at. As I argued, the movie screen is itself a looked-into medium; so it partakes of that rapt directing of attention that looking into brings. The screen entices me to adopt the posture of the voyeur, because of its looked-into character, its simulation of a private space. Very often, an intimate scene will be shot by placing the camera in such a position as to record the private happenings that take place within a closed room. This explicitly induces the audience to look *into* the room, there to observe the heedless actions of the characters observed. It really is as if we are secretly watching from a safe distance as private events unfold. Surely one of the main attractions of the screened kiss is that it offers the audience a sight they would seldom enjoy in ordinary life—a deeply private moment rendered public (and large). The people kissing have no awareness of anyone but themselves (or so the scene asserts), but in fact their actions are observed by millions—and the knowledge that this is so never comes to the characters thus intruded upon. We are visually eavesdropping, and the screen urges us on with its invitation to be looked into.

Thirdly, it is not just the bodies of the actors that open up the possibilities of voyeurism; it is also their minds. Indeed, I would say that this is what is most distinctive of screen voyeurism. As intimate witnesses of what is going on in the minds of the characters, we are able to look in on the most private thoughts and feelings of the people we observe. This is in some ways the greatest achievement of voyeurism—to observe the private mental life of someone who has no inkling that he is being observed. Some observers thrill to the prospect of views into the bedroom and bathroom, the body at its most bodily; but the film viewer can get even closer to the private world of his subject (or victim)—to his soul. The tears of the grieving mother are emblems of her inward torment, and we are permitted (for a small fee) to take in the show. The disturbing scene in David Lynch's *Mulholland Dr.* in which the main female character masturbates and weeps simultaneously is surely as voyeuristic as anyone could wish. This is raw emotional reality rendered public, the private world ripped open for all to see.

I am not saying here that the impulse to watch such scenes is necessarily immoral or shameful; it may indeed be argued that this kind of "voyeurism" is essential to all dramatic art, displaying nothing more reprehensible than the desire to know the deepest secrets of human nature. I am simply saying that the essential structure of voyeurism—the unreciprocated gaze into the private world of the other—is amply catered to by the cinematic medium.

Three

THE METAPHYSICS OF THE MOVIE IMAGE

THE STRUCTURE OF THE IMAGE

The image on the screen has, and is seen to have, various distinguishing properties: it is flat, square, made of light (colored or black-and-white), thrown onto a screen by a projector, and it moves. (It also has the property of being composed of a succession of still photographs, rapidly presented, but this fact about it is not apparent to the spectator.) These properties constitute the nature of the medium, its physical parameters. When we watch a movie, we register these properties of the medium in our consciousness, even if we do not attend to them. What is the significance of this for the movie-viewing experience? What, if anything, do these properties of the medium *mean* to the spectator? They must surely inform the aesthetic experience; but do they have any wider meaning—do they *stand for* anything, and if so, what? We see the images in a certain way in virtue of their nature, but do we also *think* of them in a specific way? Is there a meaning to their form?

I am going to assume that it is at least a plausible hypothesis that movie images have some kind of meaning in themselves (as distinct from what they are images *of*). This hypothesis needs to be tested in the light of plausible suggestions about what such meaning might be. I believe, as many others have, that the human mind often works by association and analogy, so that the impact of some particular phenomenon upon the mind cannot always be confined to the local physical characteristics of the phenomenon in question—how the stimulus strikes the senses purely in terms of its physical properties. Often, the stimulus will conjure up associations in the viewer's mind, based on its similarities to other things—as when we find that a red, red rose is *like* a lover's lips. The human mind works metaphorically, linking one kind of thing with another, so that one thing comes to have the power to suggest the other. These associations may be said to be *implicit* in the sense that the viewer could not readily articulate them; that may be what a theorist succeeds in doing when she thinks systematically about the phenomenon in question. Whether the theorist's efforts in this direction are worthwhile depends on the recognition they evoke in the viewer's mind—whether the theorist has succeeded in making explicit (and vivid) what was only implicit before. Has the theorist produced an *illuminating* account of the associations that implicitly inform the viewer's response to the viewed phenomenon? Put differently, the object of inquiry—in this case the movie image—is hypothesized to have certain *connotations,* and the task is to excavate these connotations: articulate them, systematize them, make them into a *theory.* So the question becomes what the connotations might be of the physical properties of the movie image that I listed at the outset. That is what I mean by the meaning or significance of the image. Of course, there might be no meaning at all, but my working hypothesis is that there might well be, and I propose to defend various ideas as to what the meaning is. The reader must decide whether these ideas illuminate his or her response to the medium of film.

We need to say more about the formal properties of the image in order to know what associations these properties might have. To describe the image as flat is something of an oversimplification. It is not flat in the strict geometrical sense that it has absolutely no depth. Even a patch of light is made of *something*—namely photons—that gives it some thickness, however minute. But, yes, to all intents and purposes we can describe it as physically flat. It is not two-dimensional in every sense, since it represents depth. The height and width of the image are not merely representational, but are real properties of the image, corresponding with (but not identical to) the real height and depth of what is depicted. The depth of the image, however, is entirely virtual, and is seen to be. We are not under the illusion that the screen has genuine depth (as a stereoscope can produce just such an illusion, as with 3-D films); rather, we interpret various cues on the screen as representative of a depth that isn't really before our eyes—particularly, the relative size of the image. Still, we see the image as flat in the sense that it gives no impression of ordinary perceived depth: everything on the screen seems equally far away from us as viewers.

The rectangularity of the entire screen image is obviously not seen as rectangularity in the world projected, but is rather an artifact of the circumstance that the image has edges that cut off the remainder of the photographed world.

In no sense is this shape imposed by us on the world depicted in the film; it is strictly a property of the medium. The world is understood to extend endlessly beyond the boundaries of the image.

An image made of light is devoid of texture, is perceived as insubstantial, and has the weightlessness of light. The light on the screen is not seen as some kind of pigment that stains or coats it but as a strictly temporary inhabitant of its surface, instantly removable. The light shifts constantly, effortlessly, leaving no trace of its previous incarnation, and seems as infinitely malleable as anything perceptible could be. The light *plays* over the surface of the screen, as it may play over rippling water, touching it softly and briefly. This light comes from a distant source, the projection room, and is cast through space onto the screen, which intersects it, only thus producing anything that can be construed as a representation of reality—otherwise it is merely an amorphous suspended beam. The intersection of beam and screen is what conjures the movie image into existence, as the ethereal collides with the solid.

The movie image is a moving image in two senses: (1) the light patches themselves are seen to move across the screen, and (2) they depict the movement of real objects. Patch A moves across the screen to become nearer to patch B, and we see this as a man moving closer to a woman. The pictures themselves move, and they also represent movement in the things they depict. A picture in an art gallery may also move, as when it is carried from one room into another, and there can in principle be movement of parts within the picture frame; but it does not *represent* movement *by* moving. (So the title "moving pictures" for cinema is not quite accurate—it is not the fact that the pictures themselves move that is so important, but that they can convey a sense of movement in what they are pictures *of*.) In any case, movie images are active, animated, sprightly—they get around.

SHADOWS

Now, is there anything that movie images, so characterized, remind you of? What else do you know that is flat, mobile, ethereal, and an effect of light? *Shadows*—particularly shadows of people. True, shadows result from the absence of light rather than its presence, but they are still creatures of light—weightless, projected from a light source, insubstantial, flat, and changeable. Your shadow is very much like a photographic image of you thrown onto a screen, especially if the image is black-and-white. It's shaped like you, moves like you, even talks like you. Isn't a shadow play a kind of precursor or prototype of movies? A shadow is a sort of image of its original—nature's photography, as it were—and it has the ability not only to move itself, but also to represent movement in something else. If the shadows of people and objects could be peeled off them, rearranged, stored in a can, and then projected onto a screen, then we would have a crude form of the film art. In a sense, people have been watching movies for millennia, as their shadows cavorted about them.

Shadows, in virtue of being similar to movie images, are among the associations that such images have—part of their connotation. It has sometimes been suggested, indeed, that Plato's allegory of the Cave, in which spectators are condemned to look at the shadows of objects and not the objects themselves, is not so far from a description of a modern movie audience: both are worlds of two-dimensional images, capable of enacting (without being) the behavior of real things, and perhaps equally seductive in substituting for reality itself. Movie images are shadows of the screen, but with much more detail. They are shadows cast on celluloid and then held there in perpetuity. Watching a film, then, we are subliminally reminded of the shadow world that exists all around us outside the theatre.

The shadow of a person is often taken to be a kind of immaterial double of the person, so that stepping on a person's shadow is taken in some cultures to be impolite or worse. Shadows are often regarded as eerie or uncanny, in their ambiguous status as perceptible yet insubstantial—like ghosts are supposed to be.[1] They have the form and manner of persons, but they are two-dimensional replicas of persons, tricks of light. We do not confuse them with persons, but we can see persons *in* them. They can "take on a life of their own," especially if projected by a skilled shadow actor. In other words, they have some of the attributes of persons and not others—particularly not their materiality. If you can imagine aliens consisting solely of shadows, with their own consciousness and intelligence, then these beings would have some of the attributes of persons as we know them while lacking others—they would be a lot lighter, to start with. The shadow is a potent symbol of the flesh-and-blood human being that wholly eliminates the material aspect of human beings. The shadow is a textureless, flattened being which nevertheless retains humanlike characteristics. But doesn't this sound exactly like a description of a movie image of a person?

What I want to propose, then, is that the movie image has some of the meaning possessed by shadows. The hypothesis is that the movie image (of a person) gives us a dematerialized human being—a replica of a person in immaterial form—and that this generates certain associations in the mind of the audience. The movie image incorporates a dematerializing transformation—a process that subtracts the meat of the body and replaces it with splashes of light. The material is thereby rendered immaterial.

CARTESIAN SELVES

Here we must bring that old movie buff René Descartes into the discussion. Descartes split the human being into two entities, one material, the other immaterial—the body and the mind, respectively. The body is a substance with mass and bulk, a three-dimensional occupant of space, a physical organism. The mind, by contrast, lacks these attributes, being constituted by thought: it is a weightless, intangible being, existing alongside the material body. And the mind is what the *person* essentially is—what *I* am (I merely *have* a body). Thus the essential self can in principle be extracted from its bodily vehicle, as it is in the afterlife; it can be stripped of the materiality proper to the body. Descartes's immaterial mind is, in effect, the *soul* as conceived in many religious traditions. The whole point of the soul, so conceived, is that it is *not* made of meat—solid, chunky stuff—but is constituted by something rarified and incorporeal, which is not even organic in nature. It is what would be left of a human being if you took all the materiality away—pure spirit, as it were. The Cartesian self is *anti*-matter, in the sense that it is ontologically opposite to matter. The self is revealed in its true colors only when the human being is dematerialized, as it will be after bodily death.

Now it is hard not to be struck by an analogy here—between the person as manifested in the movie image and the person as conceived by Descartes. In both cases the self is rendered in immaterial form: the image on the screen is immaterial and so is the Cartesian self. Both offer us the dematerialized self, the self without bulk and mass. Nor is the Cartesian conception just the fantasy of an eccentric philosopher; it is part of a long and deep tradition of human thought and culture, and has some claim to be embedded in our ordinary "folk psychology." It is the way people naturally think of the mind as distinct from the body: we are instinctive dualists. Now let me rush to add that this does not make it *true*. It is a very controversial question whether anything like Descartes's dualism is actually a correct description of what we are (those calling themselves materialists would deny this). But it is not controversial that this is the way people naively *think* of themselves, at least implicitly; it is part of the normal human conceptual scheme. It corresponds to the ways of thinking we naturally bring to the world, and it certainly seems suggested by the way we normally experience mind and matter. If so, it exists in our conceptual scheme to be evoked. My hypothesis, then, is that the movie image evokes this primitive dualism. When we watch a movie, seeing those immaterial images dance before us, we are tacitly subscribing to the Cartesian conception of the person. We recognize that the movie image is in some ways *closer* to the real nature of the inner self than the flesh-and-blood body is, in virtue of their shared immateriality. We have no difficulty accepting the movie image as a particularly *good* depiction of the person—apt, faithful, revealing. The material body, by contrast, belongs to another category of being entirely—the world of bulk and solidity. The movie image accentuates and highlights the self as an immaterial entity.

Light is crucial to this effect. The image on the screen is composed of light. Light is, first, *light*—weightless, free of gravity, preternaturally nimble. It shares with Descartes's version of the mind an immaterial nature. We feel gravity on our bodies, but we have no sensation of gravity operating on our thoughts and feelings—the mind feels weightless and also remarkably nimble (which is faster, light or thought?). Light is also *illuminating*—revelatory, clarifying, knowledge-producing. But this is how we think of the mind—it is the mind that sheds *light* on things. The mind is what reveals the world to us. Not surprisingly, there are many metaphors connecting light and the mind: we speak of illuminating thinkers, of bright people, of reflecting on things, of incandescent genius, of being struck by a thought as by lightning, of a sparkling mind, of the mind as a searchlight or laser beam, of a face as lit from within, of the lights going out (death), of a dull or lackluster mind, of being dim, of having a dark or shadowy character. We conceptualize the mind in these images of light and its absence, showing that we find an affinity between light and mind. But the movie image is purely a creature of light and hence taps into this association: part of its connotation is the light/mind analogy. Thus it seems particularly appropriate for the representation of persons and their mental states, because of its metaphorical power. Light is used to suggest and convey the mind.

FILM MENTALISM

These reflections encourage the doctrine I shall call *film mentalism.* This is the theory, broadly stated, that there is a significant analogy between the screen image and the mind. Probably the first proponent of film mentalism was Hugo Munsterberg, the Harvard psychologist and philosopher, in his path-breaking 1916 book *The Photoplay: A Psychological Study,* written as movies were still finding their feet.[2] Summing up his theory, he writes:

> But the richest source of the unique satisfaction in the photoplay is probably that esthetic feeling which is significant for the new art and which we have understood from its psychological conditions. *The massive outer world has lost its weight, it has been freed from space, time, and causality, and it has been clothed in the forms of our own consciousness. The mind has triumphed over matter and the pictures roll on with the ease of musical tones. It is a superb enjoyment which no other art can furnish us.*

> No wonder that temples for the new goddess are built in every little hamlet.[3]

Earlier in the book he had written: "That idea of space which forces on us most strongly the idea of heaviness, solidity and substantiality must be replaced by the light flitting immateriality."[4] And in a later essay, entitled "Why We Go to the Movies," Munsterberg writes that "the photoplay expresses the action of the mind as against the mere action of the body . . . The inner mind which the camera exhibits must lie in those actions of the camera itself by which space and time are overcome and attention, memory, imagination, and emotion are impressed on the bodily world. The photoplay of the future, if it is really to rise to further heights, will thus become, more than any other art, the domain of the psychologist who analyzes the working of the mind."[5]

Munsterberg's idea, simply put, is that the movie mimics the mind's processes by containing analogues of key psychological functions: the close-up mirrors attention, the flashback is memory, the flash forward is imagination or expectation—all this combined with that "light flitting immateriality." What we see on the screen is a kind of imitation of consciousness, a modeling of our inner landscape. Bruce Kawin expresses a similar idea in *Mindscreen* when he says: "All films are *mentally presentational,* regardless of whether they 'redeem physical reality.' The mind reaches out to film and finds its own landscape, a version of its own process."[6] Thus when mind and movie come into contact, it is like one mind finding another; we see ourselves in film—our very consciousness stretched out before us. Moreover, *only* cinema provides this kind of mental analogy—not theatre, not painting, not sculpture. The movie screen is consciousness externalized, reified. It is as if the movie screen had a mind of its own.

I have stressed the Cartesian underpinnings of this analogy between film and mind—the movie image as recapitulating the mind as Descartes conceived it. But actually this is only a stepping stone to an improved version of the theory, in which Descartes's immaterial mind is replaced with something rather different. For there is a crucial *dis*-analogy between the Cartesian self and the movie image—namely, that the former has *no* spatial dimensions while the latter has *two.* We can see the flat image on the screen, despite its intangibility, but in no way can the Cartesian self be seen—it has no spatial reality whatever. It is like an extensionless point, devoid of both size and location. Not so the image of a person on a movie screen—size and location are strenuously apparent. Admittedly, the screen image is closer to the Cartesian self than the three-dimensional body is, geometrically speaking, because two is closer to zero than three is (if we are counting dimensions); but still there is a vast ontological gap between the extensionless Cartesian self and the 2-D movie image—and this gap shows up in the fact that one can be *seen* while the other cannot. So the analogy appears faulty.

The point is well taken. What we need is not the wholly disembodied Cartesian self, unperceived and unlocated, but the idea of the *spiritual body.* In fact, we have already encountered this idea in our discussion of shadows: it is not the soul as such, conceived entirely nonbodily, but the idea of the dematerialized body. This body can be seen (though not touched) and it has a kind of spatial presence. It is the kind of body we associate with the idea of ghosts and angels, phantoms of one kind or another, spectral presences in human form. This is the idea of the human body with the material stuffing taken out of it, transformed into something impalpable. Again, I am not saying that there *are* such things in reality; I am speaking only of what populates the human imagination—myths, fairy tales, fevered hopes and fears. This is an idea that clearly has some hold on us, that insinuates itself into our thoughts, whether we believe in the reality of such things or not—and the vast majority of the human race has believed and still does. The film image of a person is analogous to this notion of the spiritual or dematerialized body.

This claim is congruent with how we perceive figures on the screen, and it is not surprising that other authors have hinted at it. Christian Metz, the French film scholar, writes that on the screen "the perceived is not really the object, it is its shade, its phantom, its double, its *replica* in a new kind of mirror."[7] Parker Tyler, the American film writer, speaks of the screen's "natural translation of bodily substances into illusory and formal ectoplasm"[8] and remarks that screen actresses often strike us as "the mirages of souls incarnate, their own shadow selves, rather than real women."[9] He also refers to this "ungirdling of the illusion of flesh, this demonstrating of the invisible existence of spirit independent of matter."[10] On the topic of cartoons, Stanley Cavell observes that

> what is abrogated is not gravity (things and creatures *do* fall, and petals are sometimes charmingly difficult to climb up

> to) but corporeality. Their bodies are indestructible, one might almost say immortal; they are totally subject to will, and perfectly expressive . . . They are animations, disembodiments, pure spirits . . . Beasts which are pure spirits, they avoid, or deny, *the* metaphysical fact of human beings, that they are condemned to be both souls and bodies. A world whose creatures are incorporeal is a world devoid of sex and death, hence a world apt to be either very sad or very happy.[11]

What are the chief characteristics of the spiritual body? When an angel appears before you, how do you expect his or her body to strike you? Not solid, certainly: there will be no tangible bulk, no footprint, and no physical trace. Odorless, too: the spiritual body has no smell, and it cannot occasion a reaction of disgust. It is idealized, both in its beauty and in its powers. It has no insides—intestines, blood, or internal organs. It cannot be damaged by ordinary contact with corporeal things. Nothing about it is redundant; everything serves a purpose. Above all, as Cavell notes, it is *unified,* not an uneasy amalgam of soul and body like mortal humans; there is no schism lying at the heart of its being. Connectedly, there is no part of it that is outside the control of the individual whose body it is: everything is subject to the will of its owner, so that disease and malfunction are not part of the deal. Nor are bodily pleasures. It is a recognizable version of the human body—it has the human form, it is *isomorphic* with the corporeal body—but it has had some of the less desirable aspects removed. There is no alienation from a body like this, no division into *me* and *it.* It is the body as transformed into another type of material, an immaterial material. There is something wondrous and magical about it; it is thrilling to behold. It is a body without the ignominy of flesh. There is nothing animal about it.

This description of the spiritual body corresponds closely to the way the body of the actor on the screen strikes us. What we see on the screen is a kind of idealized and transformed replica of a real person: weightless, odorless, unified, and marvelous. And just as the spiritual body is conceived as mind incarnate—what mind would be if it were to achieve perceptible form—so the screen image gives us the human form as a repository of human feeling and thought. This is the human form *infused with spirit.* It is the soul in the *guise* of matter, taking the form it must if it is to appear to human eyes at all. Instead of being an amalgam of soul and body, with the body calling the shots, the spiritual body promises us a type of existence in which soul is dominant, in which the body is the servant of the mind—in which, indeed, the Cartesian divide no longer obtains. Accordingly, if the movie image evokes this association in the viewer's imagination, even if only implicitly, it brings with it an entire train of ideas and sentiments that will resonate deeply in the receptive viewer. The movies constitute a kind of enchanted enactment of life governed by the spiritual body—the body of the soul, so to speak. In the flattened image, rendered in light, we see the human frame in this transformed and elevated state, in a form expressive of the soul's reality.

Oscar Wilde's *The Picture of Dorian Gray* can be seen as a kind of premonitory parable about this power of moving pictures. What Dorian sees in the portrait, after making his pact with the Devil, is precisely his soul clothed in pictorial form—the soul itself, as it really is, not concealed behind a bodily exterior. His own three-dimensional body is now completely unexpressive of his soul: nothing about Dorian the person can be gleaned from inspecting his body. But the state of the soul in the portrait is immediately evident to the viewer; the portrait acts as a window to the soul, not a shield behind which it can hide. What Dorian sees there is his spiritual body, the body that his soul really possesses—and pretty foul it is. His soul has been transported from three-dimensional space to two-dimensional art, and thereby rendered visible. But this is exactly what movies strive to achieve: the transparency of the soul to the view of the audience in the form of a two-dimensional image. And the two-dimensional image is a better vehicle for this than the humdrum body—it is simply more *similar* to the soul than the fleshly body is. The image is *designed* to reveal the soul, and it has the right formal properties to do so. The life of the soul is better conveyed by the image than by the corporeal body that sits so uneasily next to the soul. From a Cartesian standpoint, indeed, the corporeal body is positively misleading when taken as representative of the soul—a kind of sensory illusion—since the soul is another kind of being entirely. But the movie image is a more apt stand-in for the soul, for the reasons I have enumerated.

THE FACE

The face is the central locus of the spiritualizing transformation I am talking about. The face is where the soul shines through most clearly. Here is Roland Barthes on the face of

Greta Garbo: "Garbo offered to one's gaze a sort of Platonic Idea of the human creature, which explains why her face is almost sexually undefined, without however leaving one in doubt . . . The name given to her, *the Divine,* probably aimed to convey less a superlative state of beauty than the essence of her corporeal person, descended from a heaven where all things are formed and perfected in the clearest light."[12] In *Film as Art* Rudolf Arnheim rhapsodizes thus:

> Consider the face of a blond woman in a film shot: the color of hair and complexion approximate to each other as a curious pale white—even the blue eyes appear whitish; the velvety black bow of the mouth and the sharp dark pencil lines of the eyebrows are in marked contrast. How strange such a face is, how much more intense—because unconventional—is the expression, how much more attention it attracts to itself and to its expression . . . Anyone who has noticed how unreal most film faces appear, how unearthly, how beautiful, how they often give the impression of being not so much a natural phenomenon as an artistic creation—towards which, of course, the art of make-up helps considerably—will get the same pleasure from a good film face as from a good lithograph or woodcut. Anyone who is in the habit of going to film premieres knows how painfully pink the faces of the film actors appear in real life when they come on stage and make their bows after the performance. The stylized, expressive giant masks on the screen do not fit beings of flesh and blood; they are visual material, the stuff of which art is made.[13]

Even allowing for the fact that these remarks were made in the black-and-white era, they still ring true: all the effects of lighting, makeup, and magnification contrive to create a transformed reality: the face as the soul configures it. The glassy sparkle of the eyes aids this ascendance to the spiritual, by focusing attention on something so palpably removed from the dull and heavy flesh of the body. Eyes on screen manage to achieve a kind of transcendent life of their own, as pure pools of living light. The face on film is not so much a mask adopted as a mask removed—to reveal the true lineaments of the soul beneath.

BLACK-AND-WHITE

The actor-director Peter Ustinov famously quipped that he filmed *Billy Budd* in black-and-white "because it is more realistic." The paradox here is that reality, of course, is not black-and-white. But Ustinov was not speaking of *physical* reality; he meant *mental* reality. Now mental reality is presumably colorless—thoughts and feelings are not objects with color (even though we may feel blue, or red-hot with rage)—but it may yet be true that black-and-white better captures the distinctions and motions of mental reality. First, it distinguishes mind from nature, so that we *see* that human drama is not just one more natural happening: black-and-white is a way of marking off the representation of mind from the representation of matter. Logically, it would make sense to make a film in which the human characters appeared in black-and-white and the background of their actions was filmed in natural color—then the distinction between mental and physical reality would be visually marked. Secondly, black-and-white seems to correspond nicely to the drama of the mind, with its sharp contrasts, its highs and lows, its combination of light (good) and dark (evil). Black-and-white is *psychologically* realistic (ethically too—along with those inevitable shades of gray). The subtraction of color from the face aids its transformation into the soul, enabling us to forget that it was just an ordinary human visage that looked into the camera. In David Lean's superb film *Brief Encounter* the faces of the lovers, etched in merciless black-and-white, show every turn of intense feeling, every sharp moral quandary, every shade of tragedy. The bleakness of their predicament, and the stark clarity of their understanding, is perfectly captured by the chromatic austerity of the image. The soul shows its true colors in black-and-white. Color can seem like a distraction from what is going on inside, despite its appeal to the superficial eye.

DANCE

Now I see Fred Astaire dancing elegantly into the frame. The thing about Astaire is, he's light, *super*-light. His body is not some sagging concession to the force of gravity. It is antigravity. It mocks gravity. The Astaire body is hardly a body at all: it always comes sheathed in an impossible elegance, with never a muscle flexing or a sinew tensing. It is fully an instrument of its owner's will. Fred dances like an angel, literally. His human body has been transformed, by his skill and the magic of cinema, into a sprite, a pure expression of grace and dexterity. This is why it is so exhilarating to watch him dance: he simply doesn't seem human—or rather, he seems *ideally* human. Only a dematerialized body could treat space and gravity as he so effortlessly does. In a certain sense, then, dance is the essence of cinema—the most visible assertion of its ability to transform the human body. When Astaire starts to move, he releases the potential of the medium—he becomes what the image suggests that he might be, a shimmering incorporeality. He lives up to his light-constituted appearance. Freedom of movement, after all, is one of the prerogatives of the disembodied—flying angels, wafting ghosts, levitating genies. Astaire is of their happy band. His body is without mass and drag, a creature of pure movement. This ideal of dance is what the movie image itself aspires to be—a weightless vehicle of free motion.

Slow motion likewise frees the screen figure from the constraints of normal movement, rendering it weightless and exempt from physical law (speeded-up motion works similarly). In these special effects the human body takes on some of the privileges of the immaterial realm (if such there be)—it is no longer shackled to its own bulk and density. And don't we, at least in some moods, yearn for release from materiality, with its heaviness, its mutability, its mortality? (Isn't that, ultimately, what dance is all about?) The sheer inertness of matter—its essential mindlessness—can seem repulsive in itself. We want to overcome the alienation we naturally feel from our own bodies, which can seem so remote from our inner selves. We seek "annulment of the flesh."

We don't want to feel that we are made of the same stuff as the objects around us—as if we were nothing very special, ontologically. Movies offer us a transformed reality in which the body is stripped of its material bonds and becomes united with our essential nature as centers of consciousness.

CHURCH AND CINEMA

If spiritual bodies, analogous to angels, confront us on the screen, then is watching a movie anything like a religious experience? A darkened, gloomy interior; a wall blazing with light; tales of good and evil; reigning gods; a trance-like state; music; an audience—what am I talking about, a church or a movie theatre? The film theorist Dudley Andrew writes: "What of the tales told of medieval crowds weeping before a new stained-glass window or being literally entranced within the space of a new cathedral. If cinema has taken over this powerful function of art, we have come a great distance from 'Art as Technique.' "[14] Architecturally, movie houses and churches are not dissimilar, particularly with regard to the piercing of gloom by luminous pictures: the screen or the stained-glass window. Those windows are super-bright patterns of light, typically telling stories of some sort, and receiving the upturned gaze of the devotee. They tell of a world beyond and give off an aura of the supernatural. They afford visual pleasure, treats for the eye. They also transform the human body into a creature of light and radiance, as well as representing such spiritual entities as angels and prophets (as well as demons). Looking at them (or into them) is surely remarkably similar to the look invited by the movie screen. And the experience is not entirely visual; there is also a soundtrack to accompany these spiritual sights. There are hymns and sermons, organ music, chanting, just as there are words and music to fill out the visual narrative of the screen. You gaze enchanted at the glorious mosaic of glass as the plangent organ music accompanies your vision; you are transfixed by the screen as the soundtrack thunders or murmurs its message. (There is meant to be no talking, but occasionally you cannot resist a sideways comment.)

Psychologically, there is an emotional stirring, a sense of great themes, a moral focusing, and sometimes a state bordering on trance. The congregation may become so caught up in the moment that they wail and weep, overflowing with emotion; but so too in the cinema audiences have been known to faint and cry out—emotions run high there too. The power of both places to induce a trancelike state hardly needs emphasis. Both can bring their attendees to a state of transport and self-forgetfulness, seizing them at the core. Exiting the establishment can be felt as a kind of cleansing, as if dangerous energies have been released. There is even something analogous to the conversion experience that can affect the movie viewer: people often speak of the profound impact of a particular film on their worldview. Movies can be ethically and politically powerful, as much as any harangue from the pulpit. The *intensity* of the cinema and the church experience (at least on some occasions) is not to be denied. And both places seem alive with spirit, the body taking second place.

In both a cinematic and a religious experience you are surrounded by and enveloped in a complete world. Sight and hearing are fully occupied. It is not like being in an art gallery or watching television, where the object of your attention is one thing among many. You are in a space whose entire point is to fully engage your attentive faculties. This provides a total immersion in the proceedings—you melt into the screen, you are taken over by the religiosity of the place of worship. You are, as the English say, "sent." The enormous contrast between the world inside these spaces and the humdrum world outside serves to insulate you from what is not of the moment. For the duration, you are in a different zone of reality entirely, where all the normal rules seem suspended. Everything seems focused on the inner life of man, even though the world presented is preeminently a visual world. Souls flit across the screen, stirring your own soul, as souls are also the subject matter of the religious service. In church or cinema you enter into a new relationship with yourself and other people, a new level of consciousness. (Not that it is always that inspiring: there are banal and artless movies that leave you cold, as there are dull and tedious church services.)

Religion has always been concerned with processes of transformation, more or less miraculous: not just sudden religious conversion, but water turning into wine, bread becoming flesh, flesh becoming spirit (in the afterlife), God becoming man, angels turning into devils, the sick becoming whole. The notion of radical transformation seems essential to religious thinking. These transformations regularly take the form of transubstantiation, or the turning of one kind of substance into another. We clearly have a fascination with such radical alterations in a thing's nature (as the alchemists obviously did in their desire to turn base metals into gold). The movies present us with just such transformations. The idea of bodily transformation is rife in movies: people into monsters (vampires, werewolves), flesh replaced by metal *(Robocop),* children into adults and vice versa, men into women, ordinary men into supermen, people into ghosts, and so on. And then there is the general transformation of the solid substantial body into the spiritual body that I discussed earlier—a kind of analogue for the process of immortalization. Both religion and movies are fixated on these kinds of magical or quasimagical transformations. They implement what we can only imagine. They outdo the transformations of mere nature (caterpillars into butterflies, rock into lava, life into death, etc.). A part of us still yearns for that primitive prescientific worldview in which anything can happen if the supernatural forces are aligned just right.

I have already mentioned our tendency to deify the actors and actresses of Hollywood. Parker Tyler refers to them as "those modern vestiges of the old Greek divinities" and "the enlarged personnel of the realistically anthropomorphic deities of ancient Greece," noting that they are "fulfilling an ancient need, unsatisfied by popular religions of contemporary times."[15] He is surely onto something right here. It is no great stretch to see in our contemporary culture of celebrity, in our worship of the stars of the tinsel screen, a reversion to pagan religions, with their casts of gods and goddesses, often petty and embattled, fodder for obsessive speculation, larger than life, but always shiningly divine ("You look *divine* in that dress!"). Old-style religion had many gods, of distinctly human aspect, not all-powerful, representative of many human types, yet still divine, still to be worshipped and placated, still *a cut above.* The very nature of the screen image encourages this deification—the transformation it effects in the normal human body. It takes mortal aging flesh and converts it into ageless columns of dancing light. It takes the smelly human animal, all armpits and bodily fluids—hairy meat, basically—and transforms it into an Ideal Being: radiant, glistening, and sublime. No wonder these divine entities prompt our worship. The tabloids are our version of the ancient Greek myths—and are no doubt just as mythical. Perhaps the movie theatre is more like the village gathering around the raging fire, with thumping drums, witch doctors, and incantations to the gods, than the relatively staid precincts of Christian churches. Polytheistic and pagan, full of violence and conflict, sexual passion and hunger for power, the movies approximate more closely the religion of our wilder forebears: not the decorum of the stained-glass window, but the volatile violence of the bonfire. The body count of the average Hollywood blockbuster certainly equals the human sacrifice of even the most extreme pagan religious cult.

Speaking of the less tasteful aspects of the religious impulse, it would be remiss of me not to mention the corruption and mendacity that infiltrates so much religion and moviemaking. It isn't all virtue and goodness, is it? The public front is not always matched by what happens behind the scenes. The love of power, of manipulation, of privilege, the fake benevolence, the desire for riches, the concupiscence, the casting couch, the backstabbing and betrayals, the rank hypocrisy—all these amply flow in both domains. Human venality seems to thrive in these worlds of uncritical worship and dubious charisma. Certainly there is no shortage of vice behind the silver screen and the burnished altar (as well as a steady trickle of goodness, no doubt).

MENTALISM AND REALISM

Film mentalism is the view that our acquaintance with the screen is significantly like our acquaintance with our own minds; it is as if consciousness itself suffuses the screen. If the moving image is like consciousness transplanted, how can perception of it yield an awareness of things that exist *outside* consciousness? Shouldn't our awareness find itself restricted to what goes on inside the mind, instead of taking in a whole wide world? How can we be both looking into a mind and also looking into the world? Aren't the mind and the world very distinct things? Either the screen gives us the mind or it gives us the world—it can't give us both, can it?

The mind is, of its essence, directed at things beyond itself. When I see or think about an ordinary object—say, a hat stand—there is, on the one hand, the hat stand in the world that is my mental *object,* and there is my mental *act* of seeing it or thinking about it, on the other. The mental act by its very nature puts me into mental contact with an object in material reality—this is what philosophers call its intentionality. It is the idea of a mental state's being *about* something out there—having a reference beyond itself. The whole point of consciousness is not to wallow in its own juices, sealing itself up from the external world, but rather to *link* us to what lies outside ourselves—to make us aware *of things.* Consciousness is essentially a self/world linkage, a bridge between ourselves and reality. Examine your own consciousness now: you will see that it is perpetually offering up tidbits of reality to your awareness—a chair here, a cat there, a smell from who knows where. You can never catch consciousness idling within itself, taking time off from the labor of acquainting us with the world; it is always externally engaged, always plugged in. To be conscious at all is to be conscious *of* something.

But now we can see how mentalism and realism combine: the screen *has intentionality.* Those shifting images on the screen refer to things beyond themselves; and when we become acquainted with them, we simultaneously become acquainted with what they represent. We see the image of Mae West and are thereby introduced to the lady herself; her image conducts our awareness to its cause and original (this is the mechanism of embedded reference, discussed in the previous chapter). So the screen has one of the key characteristics of consciousness: making reference to things outside it—i.e., intentionality. Accordingly, when we perceive the screen, we see in the image what the image depicts. It is not, of course, that we see these objects in an unmediated way, as we do when we see objects in front of us; we see them through the good offices of their cinematic representatives. Yet we do see them. As I noted earlier, you can recognize objects by first recognizing pictures of objects—the picture identifies the object. You can find a particular man in a room full of people by being shown his picture, but being given his name alone gives you no perceptual basis on which to make the identification.

The intentionality of the screen parallels the intentionality of the mind. When I am aware of my own mental states I am thereby aware of their objects (this sensation of red I am having is a sensation *of red*), just as when I am aware of the screen I am aware of the objects it portrays (this image of a tall man is an image *of a tall man*). In both cases, we describe the referring item—the sensation or the image—in terms of what it refers to: we specify the nature of the sensation or the image by saying what it is *of*. Thus, when we become acquainted with these items, our acquaintance points through them to what they are about. Seeing the mind on the screen just *is* seeing what the cinematic image is about. Consciousness embeds the world just as the screen image does, so both bring reality into the picture (literally). Indeed, we might say that the notion of embedded reference has its basic application in the case of consciousness itself—the world of external things is embedded in my consciousness of it—and that the notion applies to the screen by analogy. The applicability of the notion of embedded reference to consciousness shows that film mentalism and film realism are compatible: your consciousness is surely mental, but it has reality firmly within its sights.

Yet the image is indisputably of a different *nature* than what it is an image of, as I have been at pains to insist. The formal properties of the image are categorically different from the properties of real objects—people are not made of light, for example. The image manifestly *contrasts* with what it is an image of. Arnheim writes: "By the absence of colors, of three-dimensional depth, by being sharply limited by the margins of the screen, and so forth, film is most satisfactorily denuded of its realism. It is always at one and the same time a flat picture post card and the scene of a living action."[16] The image enables us to see its object, but the two entities are of contrasting natures, and are seen to be so. You see the image and you see its reference, but these two perceptual objects are contrasting entities: one is two-dimensional, the other three-dimensional; one is dematerialized, the other is not; one is fixed in time, the other is not; and so on. We can say that the two entities belong in different ontological *categories.* We have no tendency to confuse the two things; anyone can see that an image on a screen is not a real person. Yet the two are placed in an intimate relationship, a kind of interweaving: as I said in chapter 2, we see each of them *under the aspect* of the other.

This coalescence of opposites can be encapsulated under the portentous title *contrastive juxtaposition.* The image and its object are juxtaposed, placed one upon the other, but they are also contrasting entities. The essence of the cinematic experience is therefore contrastive juxtaposition: the seeing of one thing in another, where the two things are categorically different. The reciprocal seeing that is characteristic of film viewing is a seeing of entities cast in contrastive juxtaposition—a kind of melding or merging of opposites. In a certain sense, then, there is an ontological *collision* here, as an entity belonging to one category abuts an entity belonging to another; or else a kind of magic trick, in which incongruous partners are made to form an indissoluble unity. The defining paradox of cinema as an artistic medium is that hard reality comes to us in gossamer form.

The flatness of the screen and the depth of the scene are a prime locus of this paradox. When the film titles are showing we are reminded of the two-dimensionality of the screen—it is like paper with writing on it—but once the movie starts the third dimension kicks in and we let the flatness retreat from focal awareness. When, at the close, the words THE END rudely decorate what was lately a locus of seething three-dimensional reality, the viewer is reminded that all along it was just a flat surface—that this was just *a movie*. But, of course, that flatness was never really forgotten, since it is etched indelibly into the perceptual impression created by the film. The depth is a kind of pretend depth, an imagined depth. We are simultaneously aware of flatness and depth—indeed, depth *in* flatness—contrastive juxtaposition. We see the image enlarge across the screen in two dimensions, *and* we see a man approach along the dimension of depth; but these are not separate acts of seeing. We can think of the screen as making a bargain with the audience: "If you ignore the fact that I am merely two-dimensional, then I will create for you a semblance of depth." Directors sometimes exploit this paradox by making the screen play tricks that advertise its flatness—for example, split-screen images or screens on screens. This jolts the viewer out of his customary acquiescence in the screen's implicit contract—now he is reminded again of the screen's existence as a flat medium. The formal properties of the screen are accented, so that the juxtaposition now highlights the image side of the image/object fusion. Normally, the screen effaces itself, but in these techniques it draws attention to itself. In this moment, the contrast that is always written into the medium is thrust upon the viewer's attention. The viewer is made fully conscious of the fact that a three-dimensional world comes to her in two-dimensional form.

Another technical feature of film that illustrates contrastive juxtaposition is the blur. The viewer hardly notices it, but in most shots the foreground is in sharp focus and the background is blurred (except where deep focus is used, as famously in *Citizen Kane*). Sometimes directors will intentionally bring a blurred image into focus before the viewer's eyes. But objects themselves are not blurred—an object doesn't really lose its definition if it retreats into the distance. In no way do we interpret cinematic blurring as a real loss of sharpness in objects—this is, we know, just not how physical reality behaves. The image and the object have contrasting properties, despite their co-presence to the viewer. What we know to be a clearly defined object is seen under the aspect of a blurred image, and a blurred image is seen as representing a clearly defined object. The blurring is taken in stride, as a formal property of the medium that coexists with the sharpness of the represented object.

Where there is a conjoining of opposites there is often irony. You say one thing and mean another, at variance with the first. Similarly, the movie image *is* one way but it *conveys* something else, contrasting with the way it is. It is as if the screen winks at the viewer when it makes its bargain: "I know, and you know, that I'm only a flat swipe of light, but I can bring to life vistas of substance and solidity." That it can do so is ironic, given its real intrinsic nature as insubstantial flatness. The uncanny ability of the screen to simulate *life*—not just inorganic movement—is likewise an ironic achievement. It seems to me that irony is at the heart of the movie-watching experience—the irony of a medium with one kind of nature so successfully conveying a reality whose nature is very different. The feeling of mismatch, of incongruity, is almost comical. Think of an old silent film, black-and-white, no voices, too fast, palpably "unrealistic": isn't it ironic that it manages to tell us so much about the real world of noisy, colored, speaking, slow-moving people? It *ought* not to be able to do this, and yet it pulls the trick off. And isn't this irony part of its charm? It is as if one is constantly suppressing a smile while watching a film—a smile of appreciation for the ingenious irony of it all. Nor is this irony lost on filmmakers, who often trade upon it to produce interesting effects, as with the split screens and screens within screens I mentioned earlier. I am surprised that no one has made a film about two-dimensional people that disappear into infinitesimal nonentities as they turn sideways to the viewer, since this is essentially what the figure on the screen is. In this light, then, we could also describe the essence of the movie image as *ironic* juxtaposition.

I think exactly the same is true of consciousness—its essence is contrastive (or ironic) juxtaposition. Although consciousness incorporates objects from the external world, it is not itself an object like those objects. Consciousness presents itself as immaterial, even as it delivers material things to our awareness. This is most apparent with respect to our awareness of space. Perceptual consciousness, in particular, delivers up a world of spatial entities—solid occupants of physical space. But this very spatial consciousness is not *itself* spatial: it is not that conscious awareness of a square table is itself square or a table! Conscious states have no size or shape, though they are *of* things with size and shape. So the essence of visual consciousness, say, is to present an objective world of spatial entities, while itself not being objective or spatial. Consciousness therefore *contrasts* with what it represents, with what is embedded within it. And this is something that self-conscious creatures, such as ourselves, are aware of—we *know* that our consciousness contrasts with the world it presents to us. Consciousness exhibits contrastive juxtaposition. Thoughts are immaterial (or strike us that way), though they are about material things; and awareness of a thought is always awareness of what the thought is about. So in this important respect consciousness and the screen are alike: the screen resembles consciousness in the way the image contrasts with what it is an image of.

We are condemned to be both confronted by a material world and yet not of that world. The world in which we live and have our being is a world of objects in space, and yet the very thing that makes this evident to us—consciousness—is itself *not* an object in space. Our nature as conscious beings stands in stark contrast to the reality that consciousness makes available to us. Without this *non*-spatial attribute we could never become aware of space. The designer of the universe must have smirked at this irony when he made it so. By designing us on the principle of contrastive juxtaposition he inserted a deep irony into the heart of our being. Indeed, our nature as conscious beings contrasts with our nature as animal bodies, since these belong to that spatial world that consciousness seems to negate. The original irony lies within our own being as embodied minds. We are spatial and nonspatial at the same time, as part of our very personhood, and the two are inextricably linked—ironic, is it not?

THE REPRESENTED BODY

I have spoken of the movie image as transforming the human body into a dematerialized medium—flat patches of light—and of the meaning of this transformation. Now I shall compare and contrast this with the way other arts transform the human body, so that we can see what is distinctive of the movie image.

Sculpture, I remarked earlier, is at the opposite extreme to the movie image: it typically represents man in heavier materials, stone and metal, as against a weightless packet of light. And it does not move. It is not the spiritual body that we see in marble but an exaggeration of the material body of flesh and bone. Yet I think sculpture can be seen as making a very similar metaphysical point to the movie image—about the contingency of our physical makeup. The same human form can be bodied forth in different materials, some heavier than others, from the flimsiest to the densest. So sculpture too can be seen as insisting on the distinctness of the human soul from the material that happens to clothe it. It affirms the spirit as something different from the body. It does so ironically, by *stressing* the materiality of the body, while at the same time showing its irrelevance to the human essence. Consider Rodin's famous *Thinker,* a solid hunk of metal lost in contemplation: surely the irony here is obvious—that *metal* might think! This serves to accentuate the point that it is surprising and ironic that *flesh* might think—that the material brain might be what lies at the base of the human mind.[17] Just as the movie image toys with the duality of human beings by dematerializing the body, so sculpture asserts the same duality by underlining our materiality, so indicating its essential irrelevance. In sculpture we see the marks of the human soul amid the heaviest and least mobile of materials, thus illustrating the ability of the soul to make its home in the most unpromising of substrates. It is really just as amazing, ultimately, that we are made of flesh as it would be if we were made of bronze.

Then there are puppets, dolls, action figures, waxworks, stuffed animals, robots, and portraits—all reworked versions of the body. Neither the movie image nor the sculpture is much like the waxwork, which really does try to replicate (visually at least) the human body—its aim is to be mistaken for the original. The waxwork shows how different the movie is from its original—how "unrealistic" the medium is. You might mistake a waxwork for a real person at a distance, but who has ever mistaken a movie image for a real person? Puppets provide an interesting case: no one would mistake them for a real person, yet they aim for a certain kind of naturalism. They resemble movie images in respect to ventriloquism: a voice is thrown into the puppet's mouth in much the same way speech appears to emanate from the mouths of those two-dimensional puppets on the screen.

The voice is pretty much a normal human voice in both cases, but the apparent source of the voice is a transformed human—large and flat in the one case, small and knobby in the other. The Punch and Judy show is not a million miles away from the film: patently unreal figures, of altered dimensions, spouting their lines—or seeming to. Both convey a startling animation, in the sense that we quickly forget that they are only *effigies* of real people; they "take on a life of their own." And I think that both demonstrate a kinship with the *uncanny*—they seem to move of their own volition, despite their lack of inner agency. It is uncanny if inanimate objects begin to move as if they had a will of their own, and both puppets and movie images do this—it is *as if* they were alive, while clearly not being so. Shadow puppets are one kind of puppet; those shadows on the screen are another kind. The difference is that puppets preserve the mass and substance of persons, while scaling them down; the image on the screen drains persons of their corporeality while scaling them up. Still, they both involve transformations of the normal human form, which serve to highlight certain aspects of what we are. Puppets often capture our pettiness and insignificance; movies strive to capture our grandeur and uniqueness.

What of 3-D movies? These approximate to the condition of visual illusion, analogous to the stereoscope (of which, indeed, they are an application), and as such they diminish the contrast between themselves and real objects. They do not produce in the viewer that complex collision between image seen and object represented which is characteristic of ordinary 2-D cinema. Accordingly, the experience of viewing them is very different, and not just because of those special optical lenses. The contrasts I have been insisting on no longer inform the inner nature of the experience, or they are greatly mitigated. One is tempted to say that it just isn't *art,* which always requires some distance between the representation itself and what it represents. The 3-D image basically spoils the aesthetic experience by ratcheting it too much in the direction of realism; it doesn't do enough meaningful transforming. It tries to be a waxwork when what we seek is a metamorphosis. Or it approximates too closely the theatre experience, with real actors before us. It is surely noteworthy that 3-D has never really caught on, especially when depicting human drama. The life of the mind is not best served by the 3-D image. If I am right about the 2-D image, this is not surprising; for the 2-D image carries its own distinctive weight of meaning, not possessed by the 3-D image. The 3-D image doesn't give us what the flat image does: a prismatic distortion, an ontological reconfiguring.

ACTING

Acting is in its very nature a play with the mind-body relation. What does an actor do? She pretends to be someone she is not, the character she is playing. But what does this pretense consist of? *How* does the actor pretend to be someone else? The answer, I suggest, is that she pretends that someone else's mind is in her body. She doesn't pretend that her body is someone else's: that would be a hollow pretense, since it so obviously is her body. The audience can see the actor's body, and they don't think she is pretending that she has a different body from her normal one. What she does is act as if that body has a different personality or character associated with it. She makes her body into a *symbol* of that other mind. The actor has her own personality and motivations, but she pretends that she has different ones; in other words, she pretends that the character's mind is hers. To do this requires an assumption of contingency: that this body *might* have housed a different mind. This must seem like a credible possibility. It has to seem possible, say, that the body of Anthony Hopkins could house the personality of Hannibal Lecter in order for this actor to play that character. We have to be convinced that that character could emanate from this body. (Here is where the art of casting comes in.) So the actor is, in effect, exploiting the contingency of the link between a particular body and the mind that goes with it. If we had no conception that the same body could express a different mind, then acting would make no sense to us. If we thought that for every body there was a unique mind, fixed and invariable, then acting would be an impossible project. Acting requires the notion of multiple minds expressed by a single body—the many characters a given actor might play. But this involves metaphysical assumptions about mind and body, to the effect that the mind's relation to the body is mutable. Maybe the reasons animals can't act (most of them, anyway) is that they have no conception that minds and bodies can be detached. To pretend that you have mental states different from the ones you actually do have requires a good deal of self-consciousness about the loose link between mind and body. In a way the actor is drawing attention to the contingency of this link, and hence bringing the mind to the attention of the audience. Acting is an exercise in metaphysics.

As the film theorist Charles Barr says: "Film shows the substance, it cannot *show* the essence, but it can *suggest* the essence by *showing* the substance. It suggests inner reality by showing outer reality with the greatest possible intensity."[18] That is, all the resources of cinema—lighting, makeup, camera placement, music, voice, background, the actor's physiognomy—can work to reveal the inner being of the character, and the medium itself intensifies the effect of mentality on the screen. The mind is *foregrounded* relative to the body, which is present to the viewer only as a wispy trace. With the body ontologically reduced, etiolated, the soul comes to the viewer in its primal form, asserting its reality in the presence of the dematerialized body. The screen actor is working with her mind, primarily; the body functions as a kind of necessary intrusion on this intimacy with the audience. The theatre actor, seen in all his bodily glory and placed at some distance from the audience, must coax his entire body into carrying the burden of his performance; his raised voice, in particular, must do a major share of the work. But the screen actor can rely on subtler intimations of interiority: if her mind is in the right place, her body will communicate what it needs to. The greater naturalism of screen acting testifies to this; the body is not something to be manipulated by the actor, as if she were its puppeteer, but automatically expresses what is going on inside. If I say that the screen actor must act as if she were an angel (or a ghost), I hope I will not be misunderstood: I mean that she must act as if her body were the very stuff of her soul. She must, in other words, overcome the mind-body dualism that is our human lot. The essential point is that the body should be recognized to enter a new state of being once it reaches the screen.

THE INNER SCREEN

I have suggested that the screen is analogous to consciousness; but what of the idea that consciousness is analogous to the screen? If there were a mental screen, then this would reinforce the analogy I am making, since then consciousness would build in a screen that we somehow inwardly perceive. That idea has indeed sometimes been defended, but I think myself that there is little to be said for it. The thought is that when, as we say, you see an object, you really see a purely inner item that is somehow displayed to you in your "private mental theatre." You don't see the world "directly," but only through the intermediary of images on your mental screen—just as with the movie screen. It is as if perception were confined to what is presented on the inner screen of the mind, with the real world hovering out of reach.

However, the existence of such a mental screen is highly questionable, and the so-called sense-datum theory of perception that leads to it is widely rejected by philosophers of perception. I won't bore my reader with an elaborate refutation of the sense-datum theory of perception; I will merely note that there is really nothing wrong with the commonsense idea that you see ordinary objects in the external world. Therefore, we need no screen on which to project those alleged mental images that are held to stand in for external objects, since the objects are capable of standing in for themselves. Moreover, what *is* this supposed mental screen—how big is it, what shape is it, what color is it? We never seem to catch a glimpse of it in its own right, as we can the movie screen; it is a purely theoretical postulate, having no phenomenological reality. There is, of course, something analogous to the screen in the action and anatomy of the retina, since the retina is a two-dimensional surface on which an optical image is projected from objects. But this surface has no counterpart in the *experience* of seeing things—it is not an element in our consciousness of things. And we clearly don't *look* at the retina when we see objects. The things we see are arrayed in the world of objective space and time; they need no mental screen to hold them before our gaze.

Even in the case of mental images (which I will consider in the next chapter) the idea of a mental screen has little to recommend it. When you form an image of a black cat, say, there is no mental screen on which this image is projected—the image simply floats in its own space. If there were such a screen, distinct from the image itself, then you ought to be able to encounter it introspectively; but you have no acquaintance with any such screen. You can, of course, form an image *of* a screen, but then this image would need to be displayed on another screen—and you have no image of *that* screen. So there really is nothing in your consciousness that compares to the screen on which film images are projected, tempting as that idea might seem at first. It would be nice for my theory if there were, but the idea seems baseless. The movie screen has some of the characteristics of the mind, at least by analogy, but the mind is not itself shaped like a movie screen—a flat surface with pictures on it. Still, perhaps it is a testament to the plausibility of film mentalism that people have sensed an affinity between mind and screen in this way. It is just that they misidentified the direction and nature of the analogy. It is not that consciousness is a movie screen internalized; it is that the screen is consciousness externalized.

Four

DREAMS ON FILM

IMAGES AND IMAGES

In the last chapter, I suggested that the screened image is analogous to the mind's representation of reality: consciousness is essentially an awareness of things outside itself, and the screen too possesses this kind of reference beyond itself. But this is still fairly general, because the mind contains states of many kinds that possess such reference—beliefs and thoughts, desires and emotions, perceptions and sensations. The mental state that most resembles the film image lies in the mind's capacity to create the *mental image.* By "mental image" I simply mean those constituents of consciousness that crop up when, as we say, we *visualize* something (see something "with the mind's eye"), as opposed to really seeing something. Visual images are a specific way in which the mind represents the world, different from sensations, thoughts, and feelings. They are also the fabric of daydreams (of course, auditory and other images may also be). Now it is a substantive philosophical question exactly how mental images differ from ordinary perceptions of things—how visualizing a face differs from seeing that face in front of you—and I don't intend to go into this fully here.[1] The key difference, for our purposes, is that when you see an object with your outer eyes, you feel yourself to be in the presence of that object: but when you see it only in your mind's eye, there is no such impression of presence—the object could be anywhere. Similarly, when you are perceiving the movie screen, you do not feel that the people and objects depicted are actually present before you; instead, they are experienced as absent—you have no inclination to think that the actors are only a few yards away from you (though their image certainly is). The image on the screen represents an absent object, just as an image in the mind represents an absent object: the objects don't need to be *there* in order for you to have a visual representation of them. The hypothesis I am pursuing, then, is that the mental image is the best mental analogue for the film image. This seems preferable, say, to the idea that the film image is most analogous to *thoughts,* because thoughts don't have the kind of sensory character that images have (unless the thought is based on an image). The film image is inherently visual in just the way a visual image is, but a thought need not be specifically visual—it can be entirely abstract or conceptual.

Dreams consist of mental images—images of absent or nonexistent things—and so they are suitable candidates to be the analogue of movie images. Movie images are like dream images. The aim of the present chapter will be to defend this hypothesis, but I want it to be clear how it connects with what I have been saying up to now: the dream theory is a specific type of film mentalism. Put in very broad terms, which I shall refine as we continue, the experience of watching a movie is significantly like the experience of having a dream. In more scientific-sounding terms, movies arouse in the viewer the same kinds of psychological mechanisms and processes that characterize the dreaming state. But I don't want simply to assume that movies are dreamlike, however much my reader may already sympathize with this view; I want to establish the view by an appeal to evidence and argument.

The suspicion that there is some sort of connection or similarity between dreams and films has been around for a long time and has struck many theorists of film as well as filmmakers. Hollywood is sometimes described as a "dream factory"; there is a film company expressly entitled DreamWorks; talk interrelating dreams and movies is rampant. Here then are some representative quotations in which the dream/film association has been explicitly made. The aesthetician Suzanne Langer, in *Feeling and Form,* writes: "Cinema is 'like' dream in the mode of its presentation: it creates a virtual present, an order of direct apparition. That is the mode of the dream."[2] Parker Tyler states that "movies are dreamlike and fantastic"[3] and that "the movie theatre is a darkness, a kind of sleep in which we dream."[4] Buster Keaton actually inserted the analogy into his movie *Sherlock Junior,* in which a projectionist falls asleep and dreams he is in the very film he is projecting, departing his body to float immaterially onto the screen below, only to return to his prone body when the film is over and he wakes up. Pauline Kael referred to Cary Grant as "the man from Dream City" (according to Roger Ebert). These remarks hardly amount to a theory, however, and as they stand are little more than assertions of intuition rather than cogent justifications. I want to propose a set of analogies between films and dreams, articulate and defend them, and then consider some potential objections to the hypothesis that movie images are like dream images. None of this will amount to a *proof* in the strict sense, but I think we will see that the points of analogy are precise and illuminating, not mere vague metaphors.

SENSORY/AFFECTIVE FUSION

Dreams, as everyone knows, are emotionally charged; they are also sensory in character—particularly, visual and auditory. But these two components of the dream are not independent of each other: they are fused together into a seamless whole. One might almost say that a dream image is a pictorial emotion—an emotion in sensory clothes. Nothing about the sensory content of a dream seems emotionally redundant, and each emotion in it has a sensory expression. The dream images have clearly been *designed* to convey—better, embody—a specific emotion. Often, in waking life, our sensory experiences have no particular affective connotation—we just see and hear what is going on around us, whether it has emotional resonance or not—but in dreams the entire point of a particular item of sensory material is to manifest an emotional meaning. The faces of dream characters, in particular, seem drenched in emotional color—sometimes lovable, sometimes fearful. Dream imagery is pregnant with strong affect: the visual is the visceral, and vice versa. It is almost as if the dream machinery's prime purpose is to find a sensory expression for whatever emotions are seething within—to transmute feeling into sensation.

But isn't this also an accurate description of what moving

pictures attempt to do? What we see on the screen is intended to engage our emotions directly. This is the sensory manipulation of emotion. A well-made film succeeds in weaving together the affective and the sensory, so that every image on the screen evokes the emotion that fits the narrative. The images convey, by means of lighting, close-ups, and editing, the emotions of the characters, and then the viewer experiences his or her emotional response to all this. The face on the screen, in particular, becomes charged with emotional significance, so that every flicker of an eyelash carries affective weight. The eyes become liquid pools of dense feeling. It is as if we are *seeing* the emotions of the characters, so entwined are the images and the feelings (at least when the movie is doing its job). The clasp of Trevor Howard's hand on Celia Johnson's shoulder at the end of *Brief Encounter,* and the images of her facial expression, along with her blithely chattering companion, seem to condense an ocean of feeling into a single sensory moment. That vision will haunt the viewer, precisely because it packs such an emotional wallop. And, of course, a film is *designed* to do this—to exhibit sensory/affective fusion. It is not like a novel, in which the emotion is generated by mere words—the *words* are not experienced as dense with emotion (though the images they evoke in the mind of the reader may well be). You do not see Anna Karenina's pain in seeing her name upon the page—those marks on paper don't look as if they are at the end of their tether. But when you see the suffering heroine's face on the screen, her emotions suffuse her features. Moreover, the distinctive techniques of cinema—as opposed, say, to the stage—greatly aid this process of sensory and affective integration. The psychological foregrounding I have spoken of works to bestow a special emotional layer on the displayed image.

Perhaps our willingness to entertain sensory/affective fusion in the case of movies is preconditioned by our acquaintance with it in our dreams: we can so readily respond to it in the cinema because we are so familiar with it in our nighttime consciousness. It is as if the viewer's mind is saying: "Oh yes, I know what this image on the screen is trying to do—my dream images do it to me every night." Just as the dream machinery picks a specific sensory content in order to make an emotional point, so the filmmaker selects his image with the same kind of aim in mind. My own dream machinery is very good at picking visual images that tap into my fear of heights, giving me some harrowing nights between the sheets, but a good action director will mimic this very talent when trying to elicit like emotions in the film viewer. It is easy for the viewer to accept this interpenetration of the seen image and the expressed emotion. The screen comes alive with feeling because of its ability to suggest the mind in visual terms. The kind of seeing we experience in the cinema is *emotional seeing*—the seeing *of* emotions *with* emotions. Eye and heart are locked inextricably together, just as they are in dreams. This is not disinterested, clinical seeing, but seeing charged with feeling.

The ability of cinema to imitate the sensory/affective fusion of dreams is a large part of its power over the viewer's mind—its power to engage and penetrate the viewer's consciousness. Dreams reach to our deepest emotions by means of sensory representations; and so do movies. The invention of moving pictures was largely the discovery of how to depict human feeling, in all its movements and vicissitudes. The still image, either in painting or in photography, could capture a time slice of emotion, a frozen moment of feeling, but only the moving image could capture the inherent dynamism of human emotion, its flows, swerves, and surges. When the image on the screen transforms and flows, it mirrors the ebb and flow of emotion, the lulls and rushes that characterize emotional consciousness. The moving screen image captures as much the movement of emotions as of physical bodies. We speak of being "moved," and the word "movies" can equally connote this type of inner movement.

The role of music in film is worth considering here. In dreams emotion comes with the territory; there is no such thing as an affect-free dream. Nor is it that the dreamer must himself *supply* the emotion merely suggested by the sensory material of the dream; the emotion is woven into the dream itself. But in viewing a film the audience must bring emotion to the screen—and this process does not always come off. It is not that in the very act of seeing the images the viewer thereby has the appropriate feelings; there are certainly affectively inert films. The film must *work* to achieve its emotional power. It doesn't have an emotional content as a result of its very structure, as a dream does. In short, you can't dream without feeling, but you can watch a movie without feeling. It is true that movies achieve their emotional effects very easily, perhaps precisely because of their ability to imitate the dream state; but it would be an exaggeration to say that the audience's emotional involvement is *integral* to them, a sine qua non. Granted this, movies would do well to boost their affective power by whatever means come to hand. How are they to create an emotional soundtrack, so to speak? The answer is contained in the question—by adding a *musical* soundtrack. For music is clearly the most reliably guaranteed medium for the creation of emotion in the human breast: play a person a tune and he is putty in your hands. Add volume, Dolby sound, and you have a surefire emotion-generator. Now couple this with the images on the screen, as well as the usual voices and noises of a film soundtrack, and you have a powerful device for pumping emotion from the movie to the audience. Music takes up the slack left by the bare image as a vehicle of feeling. The images in a dream are clearly controlled and directed by the emotional requirements of the dream; the music in a film works to signal the emotional undertow of the film, as well as to manipulate the audience's feelings. The music tells the audience what to feel, and it makes them feel it. It therefore functions to create an emotional soundtrack. The dream comes with emotion built in; film music works to supply just such an emotional dimension. Thus music aids sensory/affective fusion, by boosting the affect and weaving it into the spectacle. In effect, it makes the film experience more dreamlike.

We know very little, if anything, about the function of dreams, but it does seem clear that they can provide emotional catharsis—release, purging. This is obvious when the dream is of the wish-fulfillment kind, but even an anxiety dream can be seen as releasing pent-up fears. Emotions are inherently energetic, even explosive, and they seek an outlet; dreams seem to offer one type of outlet (sports might be thought to offer another). But isn't it also true that movies have a cathartic effect? Isn't one reason that we go to movies that they permit the expression of emotions that may be taboo or at least not catered to in our ordinary life? Horror films are a good example of this function—nameless fears, childish anxieties. You don't need to be a Freudian to believe that emotions are often repressed and seek an outlet. By producing visual images in narrative form, with an emotional theme, movies and dreams convert those repressed and free-floating emotions into visible form, giving them shape and definition. The visual becomes a way for the visceral to channel itself, thus allowing for release. Both film and dream serve, not just to represent and express emotion, but to open the emotional valves—to let emotion flow freely (and perhaps safely). Both concretize the emotions and thus give them a chance to manifest themselves in a form that allows for catharsis. Catharsis needs a medium if it is not to be totally directionless; movies and dreams both, in similar ways, provide just such a medium. You may come out of both feeling shaken and disgusted, angry or depressed, but at least you got that off your chest. Romantic longings are frequent subjects of dreams and films, and it is hard to avoid the suspicion that they are so because of their pressing and exigent nature—we just have to give them free rein *somewhere.*

SPATIO-TEMPORAL DISCONTINUITY

In ordinary waking consciousness the transition from one place or time to another is continuous—you have to pass through all the intermediate times and places. You can't just jump from one spatio-temporal location to another, as if all the places and times in between didn't exist. But in the movies this is precisely what happens: the camera can record a given scene and then leap to another place and time entirely. A film splices together all these scenes, without bothering with the intermediate locations. This is quite unlike ordinary perception, which lacks this kind of flexibility (the closest we come to it is falling asleep in one place and waking up in another, while having lost track of time). The space of movies is fractured, discontinuous; and time does not flow in its usual measured manner. Yet this is a visual world, a world of perceived situations (unlike, say, the novel). The narrative structure of film is basically the sequencing of distinct and discontinuous spatial viewpoints. Rudolf Arnheim writes: "The period of time that is being photographed may be interrupted at any point. One scene may be immediately followed by another that takes place at a totally different time. And the continuity of space may be broken in the same manner. A moment ago I may have been standing a hundred yards away from the house. Suddenly I am close in front of it. I may have been in Sydney a few moments ago. Immediately afterwards I can be in Boston. I have only to join the two strips together."[5]

These abrupt jolts of camera position, pieced together according to narrative dictates, raise a question: how do we manage to take them in stride? So much violence is done to our normal ways of seeing things that you would think our minds would rebel. We ought to be saying: "Hey, that just isn't how the world works—it simply makes no sense!" But we seem to go with the flow, or the lack of it. Why? Here is Walter Murch, addressing the question of why cuts work:

> At the instant of the cut, there is a total and instantaneous discontinuity in the field of vision . . . It is all the more amazing because the instantaneous displacement achieved by the cut is not anything that we experience in ordinary life . . . *So why do cuts work?* Do they have some hidden foundation in our own experience, or are they an invention that suits the convenience of filmmakers and people who have just, somehow, become used to them? Well, although "day-to-day" reality appears to be continuous, there *is* that other world in which we spend perhaps a third of our lives: the "night-to-night" reality of dreams. And the images in dreams are much more fragmented, intersecting in much stranger and more abrupt ways than the images of waking reality—ways that approximate, at least, the interaction produced by cutting. Perhaps the explanation is as simple as that: we accept the cut because it resembles the way images are juxtaposed in our dreams. In fact, the abruptness of the cut may be one of the key determinants in actually *producing* the similarity between dreams and films. In the darkness of the theatre, we say to ourselves, in effect, "This looks like reality, but it cannot be reality because it is so visually discontinuous; therefore, it must be a dream."[6]

Suzanne Langer is onto a similar point when she observes: "Dream events are spatial—often intensely concerned with space—intervals, endless roads, bottomless canyons, things too high, too near, too far—but they are not oriented in any total space. The same is true of the moving picture, and distinguishes it—despite its visual character—from plastic art: *its space comes and goes.*"[7] Both authors, then, are drawing an analogy between the discontinuous way space is represented in movies and the way it is represented in dreams. In dreams we find ourselves undergoing sudden shifts of position, of one geographical location to another, or sometimes coming abruptly nearer to an object or person. The dream is a sequence of scenes, stitched together according to narrative rules, but often contemptuous of ordinary spatial and temporal continuity. And this suggests, as Murch remarks, that our ready comprehension of such discontinuities in film may have its basis in our prior acquaintance with like discontinuities in dreams—we have been in such bizarrely broken worlds before, as recently as the previous night. Indeed, it is just such fragmentation that causes films and dreams to converge psychologically. Films put the mind in the same kind of state that dreams do, by virtue of their similar narrative ways with space and time.

Both variable framing and montage have analogues in the realm of dream experience. Variable framing is simply the ability of the camera to adopt different perspectives on the same scene, farther or nearer, off to the side, etc. These jumps correspond to like variations in how we depict things in our dreams—now seeing someone from a distance, now finding ourselves up close. Montage is simply another name for editing, but has been held by some (notably by the Russian director and film theorist Sergei Eisenstein) to be the very essence of the movie art—that which gives it its distinctive character.[8] For montage allows the filmmaker to impose his own imagination on photographically recorded reality, and to juxtapose images never found together in nature but possessing emotional or symbolic significance (as it might be, a wretched prisoner and a caged bird). This capacity for imaginative sequencing is surely a mark of the dream: images are strung together which have never been encountered together in perceived reality but which form a nexus of meaning for the dreamer. This enormous freedom of sequencing is certainly a notable similarity between the two, as is the expressive potential of such sequencing. The invention of montage is, in effect, the discovery of how to make dreams from celluloid—by cutting and splicing. Sequencing of experience is taken out of the hands of nature and put into the hands of a creative agent—a filmmaker or a dream generator. If you set out to invent a technology that imitated the way scenes succeed each other in dreams, then surely the moving picture, with its unlimited capacity for montage, would be the technology of choice.

Nobody teaches you to dream. You don't take Elementary Dreaming in kindergarten, and your parents don't drill you in the art of dreaming. Dreaming comes naturally to us, but it is clearly not a simple matter: a dream is a complex mental product, and it is not a mere copy of ordinary experience. As the cognitive scientists say, you have a *module* for dreaming—a special-purpose psychological device, based in brain tissue, whose output consists of spatio-temporally fractured sensory/affective narratives. Since the possession of this module is not the result of learning, it must be innate. Your genes must contain instructions on how to construct and process dreams. Dreaming is not unlike language in this respect: there is also a human instinct for language, an innately based language module.[9] Indeed, in a loose sense, dreaming contains a kind of "grammar"—a set of rules for constructing dreams. In any case, dreaming is instinctual—unlike, say, doing your taxes or knowing the succession of American presidents. It is certainly not like reading and writing, which require a laborious process of explicit instruction; so dream narratives are not like literary narratives. Even the laziest student will dream profusely, no effort required; but reading and writing a novel, say, is a major undertaking. Yet both are complex narratives.

What about movies—do we need to learn how to perceive and interpret them? Not really, even though some movie devices may depend upon learned conventions—as, say, with entering a person's thoughts by means of moving the camera toward his or her eyeball and going into a fade. For the most part, movie watching is effortless and instruction-free—you just need to observe a rapt child in front of a movie screen to see that. Those strange discontinuities we call cuts do not present a hard problem of learning for the child. No manuals or textbooks need be consulted. Somehow the mind of the child is in tune with movie structure, and this seems to occur spontaneously. Why? In watching a movie a child is exploiting the cognitive machinery already made available by the dream mechanism. The child has to learn to read before a literary narrative can be processed, but watching a film requires nothing much beyond the capacity to dream. We don't need to master conventions in order to interpret pictures, so photography—including the moving picture—can be processed on the basis of the innate capacity to perceive. But the fractured character of the sequencing of these images also poses no special educational challenge because of its antecedent presence in the dream. The "grammar" of films recapitulates the "grammar" of dreams, which is written into the genes.

REALISM AND FANTASY

When we describe something as dreamlike we often mean that it bears little or no relation to reality—that it is entirely a product of imagination. Thus we distinguish imagination from perception and locate dreaming in the imagination. To be dreamlike is then taken to mean being fantastic, in the sense of a mental product that is divorced from the mundane world. In this way of thinking, my claim that movies are like dreams may appear implausible, for surely many films are "realistic"—historical epics, domestic dramas, and romantic comedies. Not all films are fantasy films. Isn't there something irreducibly *documentary* about film? After all, as I argued in the previous chapters, we do see real people when we watch a film—there is a realism to film that cannot be denied. How can films be both dreamlike *and* realistic?

The answer to this question should be obvious: in *that* sense dreams are not dreamlike, either! For it is simply not true that dreams are always totally divorced from reality, mere fantastic ravings with no input from the dreamer's ordinary waking life. On the contrary, as Freud was not the first to point out, dreams are generally firmly rooted in the normal life of the dreamer—his experiences, concerns, and obsessions. We generally dream about people we know, in situations like those of real life, and with emotions bearing an intelligible relation to our daytime emotions. What the dream does is *elaborate* on these familiarities—it takes them as a starting point and weaves a fictional narrative around them. I recently had a dream in which I met Vladimir Nabokov and had a very pleasant conversation with him about his great novel *Lolita*. I was happy to show off my detailed knowledge of his text, and together we perused a highly embossed edition of the book that looked like it had been typeset in a medieval monastery. There are obviously clear elements of fantasy in this dream, but equally clearly it is based on my admiration for the author and the fact that I often teach a course in which *Lolita* is studied. What a dream does is combine memory with imagination, in about equal proportions. Moreover, *during* a dream there is nothing "dreamlike" about it—there is no sense that we are dwelling in a land of fantasy. On the contrary, even the most bizarre dream strikes us, *while dreaming it,* to be the purest reality: dreams don't *seem* like dreams—not at the time anyway. Dreams appear real, and parts of them are indeed drawn from real life. It is therefore essential to the dream theory of cinema that films should *not seem like dreams.* If they did, they would not be experienced as dreams are—as a piece of reality. Films are indeed generally experienced as unlike dreams, but so too are *dreams* experienced as unlike dreams. The categorization of a dream *as* a dream is a retrospective matter; it is not part of the dream experience itself.

Surrealism has muddied the waters here. When you look at a surrealist painting or watch a surrealist film sequence (such as Salvador Dali's dream sequence in Alfred Hitchcock's *Spellbound*), you have the impression of something fantastic and removed from waking reality—melting watches and all that. But this is not what a dream feels like *from the inside*—as I say, it feels real. The surrealist image at best captures what a dream seems like in recollection—or at least an artist's rendering thereof. So the point of the dream theory of movies is *not* to maintain that all movies are like surrealist paintings; it is, on the contrary, to maintain that films have the thudding reality that is so typical of the dream worlds we experience ourselves as occupying. Dreams seem real, not surreal. Nor are dreams experienced *as* symbolic, in some Freudian or other sense. (Whether they *are* in fact symbolic is another matter.) Dreams strike us, in having them, as literal depictions of a real world—even when they consist of entirely fantastic people and things. This, indeed, is an essential part of their power. A good dream painting would strike the viewer as totally real while being actually fantastic—which is probably impossible. Only the sleeping mind, with its preternatural credulity, can interpret the wildly imaginary as if it were solid fact.

The important point is that a dream is really an ingenious hybrid of fact and fiction. It is suspended between two poles, wherein it achieves its delicate balance of real and unreal. One pole is remembered reality—ordinary experience imported into the dream landscape. The other is creative imagination—what the dream machinery does with remembered reality in the way of elaboration and distortion. It is part reproduction and part recombination. Here are the familiar people, the familiar places, the familiar tasks; but they are imaginatively recombined, producing strange and bizarre situations. I once dreamed that my wife took three paces in our waterlogged front yard, with each step sinking deeper into the mud, until at the third step she completely disappeared into the ground. This was all solid documentary stuff—the yard can become a complete bog—except for the fact that she so dramatically vanished. And, of course, it all seemed shockingly real at the time. The dream content is invariably this mix of known reality and conjured unreality—a distorted echo of the real.

A movie, too, is essentially a hybrid form, a mix of reality and fantasy, fact and fiction. The camera plays the role of memory, importing a literal record of reality into the proceedings—it stamps the film with the mark of authenticity (so it is unlike a cartoon). Because of the camera's memory—its storing of images of real things—it can inject into a film elements drawn from the real world, so that it is essentially documentary in its mechanism. The camera is, after all, just a dumb recording device. What lifts the products of the camera above mere reproduction is the way it is handled and its images sequenced. A movie is, at base, photography plus montage—and these components have their precise analogues in the memory and imagination that characterize dreaming. What a film presents to an audience is therefore the same sort of blending that a dream presents to a dreamer: first, reality reproduced; second, reality reconfigured. The mental faculties that go into producing a dream include perceiving/remembering and imagining; but producing a film involves the same basic combination—the camera as perceiver and retainer, with editing as the method of recombining. In calling movies dreamlike, I am not neglecting their roots in photographed reality; on the contrary, I am insisting on this element of their content, because dreams too are firmly rooted in perceived reality.

From this perspective, we can see that there is no conflict between a realist and an expressivist view of film. Yes, the movie is a medium that makes direct contact with reality, in virtue of the mechanism of its production; but it is also a vehicle for expressing the imaginative vision of the filmmaker. The film is a story told in images, a fiction woven from shards of reality: it both reproduces the world and reimagines it. But this mixture of realism and expressivism is precisely characteristic of the dream; and indeed the two working together are what power the dream: the dream is rooted in perceived reality, but it is also the expression of the dreamer's own imagination—a creative filtering of emotion. The fact that the film image results from mechanical recording in no way negates the status of film as a creative medium, no more than the fact that dreams use images from waking life negates their status as creative products of the human mind. Both types of experience gain authenticity from their reproductive component and imaginative satisfaction from their creative component. They defamiliarize the familiar, bestowing a kind of glowing freshness upon it, a creative glaze, but they do so only because they stubbornly retain and celebrate the familiar.

Some directors trade on the bipolarity inherent in film. They see that the essence of film is reality reimagined and they build upon it. Alfred Hitchcock and Steven Spielberg delight in finding the extraordinary in the everyday. What begins as a sullen and routine road trip, all gas stations and mangy motels, turns into a phantasmagoria of psychosis and shock *(Psycho)*. An ordinary night in a suburban home, cocooned in the comfortable bathos of bourgeois life, finds an undeniable alien from outer space loitering around the house *(E.T.)*. The mundane is seen to harbor the extravagant; fantasy worlds adjoin the tin and tarmac of quotidian being. This conjoining of the reassuringly familiar (if numbing) world of everyday life with the startlingly fantastic worlds of inner space (psychosis) and outer space (extraterrestrials) marks these two directors' work. This is nothing more than a reflection of the twin principles of cinema itself—realism and fantasy. Cinema takes the everyday and bathes it in fantasy, so that the viewer is made to see the world anew: imagining with the eyes, as you might say.

EXPRESSIVE NARROWING

Language contains enormously flexible modes of expression. A novel can call upon the full range of these resources to describe characters and scenes. We take this for granted, but it is really quite remarkable. A novel might begin: "Mary used to think a lot about love, lying like a starfish on her bed." Here we have a use of the past tense, to inform us of Mary's previous actions and thoughts, a psychological ascription of a particular content to those thoughts, and a metaphorical description of her specific style of lying on the bed, suggesting perhaps a certain abject longing. All this within a mere fifteen words. Language can tell us directly what a character is thinking and feeling; it can refer us to the past and future as well as the present; and it can liken one thing to another for literary effect. Contrast this with what the pictorial image can convey and not convey: all we could muster to start a film about Mary would be a shot of her lying on her bed, limbs akimbo. To indicate that this was a habit of hers we would have to repeat the shot a number of times, and to reveal her thoughts we would need recourse to speech, either voiceover or conversation; the metaphorical associations of the word "starfish" would be unavailable to us. The visual image can only take in what is happening now to the outside of a person; it cannot go straight inside to the mind and range back and forth through time. To achieve these effects it must resort to indirect methods, such as flashbacks and flash-forwards. The directness and economy of language are not available to the visual image. Nor can it easily abstract away from irrelevant features of a scene to give us an isolated detail. The visual image always offers up a totality of details.

The camera records all that is in front of it at the time of filming, whereas language allows us to describe a far wider range of conditions. A picture may be worth a thousand words, but a mere dozen words can often convey what no number of pictures can convey. The inherent restriction to the exterior present of the photographic image can be described as expressive narrowing. It is not that this is necessarily a defect; it may well be that the focusing on the present that it allows provides an especially dense and rich representation of what is happening *now*. This kind of point has an immediate bearing on the question of adapting literary works for the screen, and indicates some of the likely problems (as Jonathan Miller has pointed out),[10] such as conveying the metaphorical texture of a novel or exploring in detail the mental life of the characters. The representational powers of language make it a different *kind* of medium from film.

Is it not also true that the dreaming consciousness is likewise confined to the present tense? The dream deals with events as they happen now; there is no reference to the past and the future. In ordinary waking consciousness we have three tenses working simultaneously: we experience the present and form thoughts about it, but we also, through memory, have thoughts and feelings about the past, and on top of that we have expectations about the future. Normal human consciousness is a stew of tenses, as the present evokes the past and foreshadows the future. We are often admonished to live more in the present, the presupposition being that we also typically live in the past and the future. Our consciousness is a complex, shifting interweaving of past, present, and future. But in the dream our consciousness is stripped down to the present: we don't find thoughts of the past and future mingling with thoughts of the present. It is all very contemporaneous. There is, in other words, expressive narrowing with respect to tense. Perhaps this is part of the reason why dream experience seems so intense—the present is undiluted by the past and future. Dreaming is very much of the moment and in the moment. If this is right, then dreaming and movies have a further property in common: the focus on the present time. Both are imagistic, after all, and the image cannot exceed its inherent expressive limitations. There is a kind of crude immediacy to the way both dreams and movies represent the world, in contrast to the multilayered sophistication of language. To put it another way, you don't, in dreaming, find your mind wandering from what is currently assailing it to thoughts of what you were doing yesterday or might do tomorrow; you are fully caught up in the present. In this way your mind is as temporally fixated as the camera.

The question of dreams and psychological ascription is a little less straightforward. It is true that in dreams you have images of people's bodies and these images do not directly reveal what is true of them psychologically; so the dream is like film in this respect. But it is also true that you don't seem to *infer* the mental states of your dream characters from their behavior. How, then, are the mental states of dream characters represented in dreams? This question takes us to the topic of the next section.

OTHER MINDS

In ordinary life a human body looms into your visual field and your task is to figure out what is going on in the associated mind. You do so ultimately by observation of the other person's behavior, including his speech. Your knowledge here is inferential: you infer from the person's behavior that he is in such-and-such a mental state, and you may infer wrongly—as when you infer, say, that the person believes the money is under the mattress when he is in fact lying about it and believes no such thing. But when you read a novel the author simply *tells you* about the mental states of her characters, and she is the ultimate authority. The author *stipulates* what the mental state of her characters is, she doesn't have to discover it; and you can rely on her stipulation. Thus, if the author informs you that Mary used to think a lot about love, you *know* that Mary used to think a lot about love—you don't have to infer it from her behavior. There is no other-minds problem about fictional characters, as there is about real people, no problem of how to be sure that they have the mental states they are represented as having; and the basic reason for this is that fictional characters have the characteristics, mental or physical, they are said by their author to have. Real people, by contrast, may not have the mental states they purport to have; it is always a mere *hypothesis* that they have the mental states you think they have. Fictional characters have no narrative-independent being; they are as they are narrated to be, and we readers know their minds by knowing what the narrative says. There is none of that unsatisfactory business of making shaky inferences from the person's external behavior. It is literally inconceivable that, contrary to Tolstoy's assertions, Anna Karenina never loved Vronsky anyway.

But how does it stand with the minds of characters in dreams? How do we know *their* minds? One possibility is that we dream of bodies exhibiting certain behavior and then we infer what the underlying states of mind are: you know that a certain figure has malicious intentions toward you in your dream because you observe his behavior and interpret it as menacing. But that, surely, is wrong: rather, the malicious intentions are *given* in the dream. What you do is dream *that* the character has malicious intentions—this is a matter of stipulation within the dream. Hence you *just know* what the mental states of the characters are, because that is simply what the dream declares them to be. It is rather as if you are having a daydream and stipulate within it that someone has amorous feelings in your direction; you cannot be wrong about this, because the character is, by hypothesis, a fictional character of your own creation, who simply has no reality beyond what you endow her with. So there is really no problem of knowing other minds within dreams: the minds of dream characters are as evident as their bodies.

Most of this is quite obvious, but it has some interesting consequences. It means that there is psychological foregrounding within dreams: the minds of others are laid open for the dreamer to see, part of the dream's furniture, so to speak. The dreamer is living in an environment of other minds, as palpable as the bodies that pulse therein. It is not a matter of conjecture what the people in my dream are thinking and feeling (unless, of course, I stipulate that *this* is so); it is as obvious as anything else about the content of the dream. There is no sense in which the minds of the characters are less accessible than their bodies—just as with the characters in novels. But, further, there is a kind of union of mind and body in the dream, in that the two are precisely tailored to one another: the body I dream of is *designed* to express the mental states my dream specifies the person to have, and the mind is fully reflected in the body. The faces of the people in dreams are transparent portals to their minds; they are souls made flesh. The distortions we often find in the bodies of people we dream of are typically the result of modifications designed to express whatever the prevailing psychological profile may be. The usual gap between mind and body is closed in the dream: the physical matter of the body has dissolved into a plastic material more suitable for expressing mentality.

This must remind us of the notion of the spiritual body, as discussed in chapter 3. This is the notion of a body moved as close to the mind as it can be without ceasing to be a body. The bodies of dream characters are schematic, symbolic, and mentally saturated. They are products of the imagination. These are bodies that form no impediment to knowledge of other minds—they are not epistemological barriers to be surmounted. Instead, they are the living expression of personality, souls incarnate. Thus dreams afford us a kind of psychological presence not found in our ordinary perception of the heavy, fleshly bodies of real people. But then, given what I said in chapter 3 about movies and the spiritual body, there must be a kinship between the experience of the dream and the experience of a movie: both offer us this enhanced psychological presence, this mental foregrounding, this dematerializing of the body. In both we experience the sense of intimate acquaintance with the interior life of others. We feel ourselves to be in the immediate proximity of other minds, as if minds are shining out at us. The body has been systematically transformed into a vehicle for the expression of mind. Emotions, in particular, seem to reach right out to us, as if exerting a magnetic force on our minds. The usual asymmetry between knowledge of our own mind and knowledge of other minds is abrogated or diminished; now the minds of others are as transparent as our own. When we watch a film, therefore, the experience mimics the kind of mental acquaintance that characterizes the dream—other minds exert a kind of direct pull over our own. The shell of the corporeal body has been cracked, and the white nut of human consciousness gleams in the light. One might almost say that other minds merge with one's own.

MOVEMENT

J. Allan Hobson, the doyen of sleep science, reports that experiences of movement are very frequent in dreams, and the subject's motor cortex is detectably activated (despite the sleeper's own passivity). Such movements are commonly associated with corresponding emotions, as with a dream Hobson reports of parachuting: "The impending doom of such dream movement is typical and suggests not only the co-activation of anxiety in the limbic brain, but also the generation of unfamiliar or intrinsically impossible movement patterns at the level of the brain stem itself, where the neurons controlling body position in space are located."[11] This observation can be confirmed by every reflective dreamer: we are all extremely familiar with the way dreams incorporate movement in their content—flying, running, falling, traveling, and so on. Dreams are *hyperkinetic*—we are always on the move in them. I myself am forever dreaming of hazardous car journeys in which for some reason I find myself driving a car from a position where I can't even see the car I am driving! Thwarted journeys and impeded motion are staples of the anxiety dream, as unprecedented freedom of motion, such as flying, can accompany elation dreams.

We never seem to sit still in our dreams, do we? And all this frenetic movement is interwoven with corresponding emotions. The transformation of the body is often implicated in this, as the body becomes light as air when it takes flight. Dreams are replete with sensations of our own motion, as well as sensations of ordinary objects.

You know where I am going with this: what is a motion picture if not an extravaganza of movement? Just think of all those pratfalls, car chases, fights, journeys, and dances you have seen at the flicks. Especially with today's special effects, movement has never been more richly explored in movies. The *Matrix* movies are elaborate hymns to hurtling, leaping, and speeding. Dance is uniquely suited to film, as I noted in the previous chapter, because film can accentuate its freedom and lightness. In movies human bodies are super-active, antigravitational. And even when the main trunk is comparatively motionless, the eyelids may still massively open and shut in the close-up. All this movement is connected to emotions—fear and anxiety, euphoria, desire. The movie art is largely the science of converting feeling into action, making movement the bearer of emotion. But then the analogy with dreaming is obvious: both strongly stress the sensation of movement. In both the level of movement goes up a notch, compared with that of ordinary life; the static is shunned. The space of film, like the space of dreaming, is essentially a *motor* space, a space through which human bodies and other objects move. Therefore, the movie experience taps into the same states of mind and brain that characterize dreaming; the excess of motion simulates the dream state.

The first feature film I ever saw, *The Wizard of Oz,* is *about* a dream: the main color section simply is Dorothy's dream. Her house hurtles through space, hoisted by a tornado, lands in Munchkinland, on top of an unfortunate witch, and there she begins a journey along the yellow brick road. As she dances down the road, red ruby slippers sparkling, the movement never ceases, with flying witches, a stumbling straw man, an ambling lion, a halting tin man, and airborne monkeys. The entire film has the hyperkinesis of the dream, even ending with a balloon flight. The theme of an anxiety-ridden journey, full of obstacles and delays, is utterly dreamlike—and, of course, it *is* a dream. This emphasis on movement is typical of nearly all films; it belongs to their intrinsic appeal. The exaggeration of movement found in Asian martial-arts films is part of the same tendency—magnifying movement to dreamlike levels of intensity. Perhaps we accept such a palpable lack of realism because our dreams too violate realism when it comes to motion. We are really quite familiar with flying bodies because they are among the routine realities of the dream world; it is only in the waking hours that bodies move so frustratingly slowly and carry such dead weight. The dematerialized body is a far fleeter thing.

GENRES

Think of Arnold naked. He, the Terminator, has just materialized from the future, and he crouches in a parking lot without a stitch on. He walks into a biker bar, attracting many a disapproving and incredulous stare, there to be threatened by a big tough leather-clad bruiser ("Bad to the Bone" pounds in the background). Instead of being thrashed, as you might naively expect, he stops the bruiser's fist in his open hand and crushes it till the bones crack. He then takes the vanquished guy's clothes and calmly exits, ready to begin his appointed Terminating. It's classic Schwarzenegger—but it's also classic dream material. Haven't we all had a dream of inappropriate nakedness, of turning up at school or work improperly clad? We feel an obscure anxiety, not quite sure what we are doing wrong, only to realize that no one else is thus attired. That is Arnold the Terminator, an innocent robot from the future, not clued in to human conventions of robot couture. But he doesn't cringe and collapse: he reverses the situation completely, imposes his superhuman power on his tormentor, and comes out of the encounter with a nice new set of duds. He goes from anxiety dream to the most flagrant wish fulfillment—from weakness and vulnerability to overpowering strength. He gives us both types of dream in one scene.

Dreams no doubt come in many categories, but surely the principal two are anxiety and wish fulfillment. There are feel-scared dreams and feel-good dreams, nightmares and pleasure domes. We are relieved when we wake from the former and disappointed when we wake from the latter. Both are fantasies, exercises in unreality. Why we have such dreams is hard to say, but it is a fact that we do. This raises the question of whether movies divide into categories in a similar way: do the genres of movies match the genres of dreams? The nightmare finds its obvious counterpart in the horror film, with its monsters, psychopaths, and vicious little insects. I often have insect dreams, and films about an insect menace particularly creep me out. But the huge popularity of horror films, from the very first days of cinema—from *Nosferatu* to *The Exorcist* to *The Ring*—testifies to their deep resonance in the human psyche. Movies seem uniquely *suited* to the making of horror films, as if this is part of their destiny, and the similarity between movies and dreams makes this intelligible: movies by their nature are like dreams, and nightmares are a salient type of dream. The way that movies as a medium seem to dabble in the supernatural—with their dematerializing tendencies and violation of the laws of nature—makes them naturally adapted to the depiction of ghosts, vampires, werewolves, and all the rest. The horror film, in its many forms, is an enduring and immensely popular genre of film; it answers to the lowbrow in all of us, the shivering, childlike, irrational dreamer. Surely, this is the area of overlap between dreams and movies that has been most self-consciously exploited by filmmakers—they *know* they are putting nightmares up on the screen. The kind of terror they evoke is not the rational terror of ordinary waking life—wars, crimes, accidents—but the irrational fantasy terror of dream life. I doubt that if we never had nightmares, horror films would engage us in the way they do now. Hence the retort many a parent has made to a distressed child: "It's only a dream" or "It's only a movie."

The feel-good dream also has its movie counterpart. Many dreams involve the realization of our wishes. The romantic comedy or simple love story, in which all's well that ends well, clearly echoes the dream of romantic fulfillment, chaste or otherwise. But pornography, more or less hard, finds a ready partner in the sex dream, also one of the most common and well attested. The gratification of the sexual impulse is clearly something that both movies and dreams are particularly good at. The porno flick is simply the wet dream on celluloid—let's make no bones about it. Here the genres of film and dream match up neatly and precisely. In the case of violence, the situation is interesting, because the real theme of so many violent films is actually the empowerment of the powerless—think here of Clint Eastwood's *High Plains Drifter,* which carries a strong whiff of the dreamlike about it. In a dream you may be assailed by ruthless and vicious aggressors, and when the dream is of the feel-good variety it ends with you managing to assert yourself over them—*they* end up vanquished. You may do a fair amount of damage in your dreams, in overcoming the bad guys—it's not always pretty. But this is the theme of numberless revenge movies: the weak are abused, made victims of unjust violence, but they, or their no-name savior, in the end visit righteous retribution on the evildoers. I could cite many examples of this theme, but Sergio Leone's *Once Upon a Time in the West* stands out, a film in which Charles Bronson delivers a beautifully contrived comeuppance on the spectacularly nasty Henry Fonda. This kind of righteous violence is pure wish fulfillment—the desire that evil shall be put down and justice be done. (That it is often oversimplified does nothing to reduce its psychological power.) So there is a match here between the wish-fulfillment dream and the movie of justified vengeance.

THE BASE SELF

Movies have never been, with rare exceptions, a highbrow medium. They rejoice in the visceral, the gaudy, and the vulgar. And this has been held against them by critics who prefer the still gray matter of the brain to the whirling kaleidoscope of the screen. To be sure, there have been art-house movies, with big words in them, and obscure plots, and little in the way of rush and throb; but this has always been a minority taste—movies today are as philistine as they have ever been. Movies revel in sensation and emotion (often the cruder, the better); deep abstract thought is not their thing. They are a sensory (and sensational) medium, inarticulate, nonverbal, dazzlingly in love with spectacle (the circus is not dissimilar). Brutality and disorder, death and destruction—these are their frequent themes. There is nothing more cinematic than the sudden shock of a fearsome predator lunging into the screen, eliciting a gasp of surprise from the audience. Even a "sophisticated" filmmaker such as Ingmar Bergman deals in raw emotion, conflict, and violence of the spirit. This is surely why those of a certain cast of mind have always disapproved of the movies (as they have rock music and, before that, jazz). They rightly sense the anarchic flow of some of our most—what shall I say?—*basic* emotions (I won't say "animal" because animals don't in general enjoy explosions and knife fights). They correctly discern that movies don't as a rule engage the higher mental faculties.

However, I am here not to condemn this trait of film, but to explain it. Sleep science has shown that the brain is selectively activated during dreaming: the parts that control sensation, emotion, and movement are as active as they are in the waking state, but the parts that sustain reasoning and self-reflection are dampened down. Thus J. Allan Hobson writes: "We can see that, when the brain self-activates in sleep, it changes its chemical self-instructions. The mind has no choice but to go along with the programme. It sees, it moves, and it feels things intensely but it does not think, remember, or focus attention very well."[12] Later he says: "The *reason* that dreams are so perceptually intense, so instinctive and emotional, and so hyperassociative is because the brain regions supporting these functions are more active. The *reason* that we can't decide properly what state we are in, can't keep track of time, place, or person, and can't think critically or actively is because the brain regions supporting these functions are less active."[13] Now these results from the study of the dreaming brain must pique the interest of the student of film, for they are eerily reminiscent of what is obviously true of film. Just as the higher intellectual and critical faculties are diminished during dreaming sleep, so the movie watcher is operating at a psychological level at which the higher mental faculties are not in play or are in abeyance. The parts of the brain that are most active in movie watching are connected to sensation, emotion, and movement; and these crowd out the more abstract conceptual functions of the brain. If we call the parts of the brain that are responsible for sensation, emotion, and movement the SEM brain, then we can say that in movie watching it is the SEM brain that is primarily recruited; the critical and reflective faculties are (largely) offline.

Here I want to bring in the idea of the "base self"—the

self that is childlike, instinct-driven, and sensation-fixated. This I distinguish from the critical self, which is reflective, language-driven, and conceptually fixated. (Think Jekyll and Hyde, roughly.) My hypothesis is that the base self is uppermost in the dreaming state (the self subserved by the SEM brain) and is also calling the shots in the movie theatre, while the critical self takes a well-earned rest. To put it more pointedly, the crassness of movies is a function of the brain regions that are activated during them, which overlap with the regions of the brain that are active during dreaming sleep. Can we *explain* the lowbrow character of movies by the fact that it is the dreaming brain that is primarily activated by them? As the physiology of sleep tells us, the brain can be selectively activated, with some parts active and others quiescent. According to the present hypothesis, in the movies the brain likewise shifts its patterns of activation. The preoccupations of the sleeping brain—fear, appetite, wish, and delirious fantasy—are also the preoccupations of the mass movie audience. The movies chemically alter the brain in the direction of its dreaming mode: that, at any rate, is the hypothesis. During sleep the SEM brain wakes up, as it were, and with it the base self, while the critical self snoozes; I am suggesting that something similar might be true for the state of semisomnolence known as watching a movie (later I will consider whether the fact that the movie viewer is technically awake alters the picture).

Unfortunately, there is no hard scientific proof as yet that the brain is functionally similar in the dreaming and movie-watching state; the empirical work simply hasn't been done. I commend this as a research project for some eager young sleep scientist. But from ordinary observation it seems tolerably clear that the brain of the movie watcher must be functioning differently from how it does in ordinary situations: the sensory stimulation from the screen is quite different; the emotions are typically aroused and coursing, though not leading to the usual behavior; the imagination is strongly activated; the body is still; the attention is absorbed; you are not usually thinking about that broken pipe or the stock market or early retirement. Also, there is a sense that one's own psychic landscape is being explored, sensitive areas probed, shameful truths exposed. Dreams and movies are both voyages into the land of unruly emotion, excavations into the self (the base one). There is a sort of psychic clarity to both, a heightening of perception. Leonardo da Vinci reportedly asked, "Why does the eye see a thing more clearly in dreams than when awake?";[14] and the same thing can be said about movie watching. In both states the varnish comes off reality; there is the feeling of truths being revealed. Just as people's dreams are keys to their real selves, their deepest longings and anxieties, so their taste in movies tells you a lot about them. Is this why people are often ashamed of the kind of movie they like? One person might speak of his "weakness" for horror films or soppy romances. Another might be a sucker for patriotic war films. Quentin Tarantino obviously can't get enough of acrobatic violence. And how many people do you know who will proudly confess to a passion for the *Death Wish* series? I personally can watch almost anything with vampires in it—or Denise Richards suitably attired.

Let me add one small piece of anecdotal evidence. It is

said that Ludwig Wittgenstein used to like to go to the flicks after a particularly grueling philosophy seminar; sitting in the front row, he would revel in the latest American gangster film or cheesy western. Since Wittgenstein was an unusually intense thinker, with a fierce critical intelligence, one might surmise that the movie experience afforded him some release from this part of his brain—it effectively shut down the part where he did his excruciating philosophical thinking. The Wittgenstein SEM brain could then enjoy a holiday from its overactive critical duties. And I have to say that I experience movies in just this way myself. There is nothing better after a hard day of philosophical thinking and writing than a "mindless" movie; I can almost feel my brain shifting its chemical balance, the neurons rearranging themselves. It can be hard to shut down the severe critical self, and movies work to push it aside in favor of more elemental concerns. The base self must have its day. Dreams and movies put us in touch with parts of ourselves that may not have much outlet in the civilized and restrained world we mainly inhabit.

THE MIND'S LAWS

The laws of the actual physical world are not the laws of the movie world; the movie world conforms rather to *psychological* laws. The movement of the camera mimics the directing of attention, and the sequencing of scenes respects the psychological needs of the narrative, not the constraints of space and time (spatio-temporal discontinuity is really psychological continuity).[15] The succession of film images is driven by psychological forces, not physical ones. Psychological association and narrative necessity govern the way that cinema shows us the world. The laws of film are psychological laws, of the kind manifested in dreams, not physical laws. In dreaming the mind leaps from image to image, pursuing its own inner logic, dancing to its own tune; and movies do much the same thing—they arrange reality to suit the demands of mind. If we think of a dream as a kind of inward composition, then dreams and movies can both be said to follow the laws of the mind. Both involve the compacting of feelings into sensations, according to the dictates of the mind's own agenda. If the mood calls for a sudden release from gravity, or instant aging, or otherworldly beauty, or a man becoming a beast, then movies and dreams will perform the necessary magic. They don't give a damn that these things are physically impossible; all they care about is that they are psychologically indicated. "Magic" is, indeed, one of the stock words used to describe the workings of film, thus suggesting a freedom from natural law; but a similar magic is wrought every night in our dreams, which likewise flout the laws of nature regularly. This is why neither is just a recording of reality; they are a reshaping of reality, according to psychological requirements. They are products of the imagination, and the imagination is not constrained by what nature throws its way.

This independence from natural law also gives to dreams and films a marked sense of freedom. In both we can see the human will at work, following its own peculiar (and sometimes obscure) logic. There is no slavish adherence to the senses, but free creation—the mind in flight, so to speak.

There is exhilaration to both, as if we can leave the world of law-governed matter behind. And movies frequently exploit this sense of exhilaration, particularly in flouting the laws of motion. Movies and dreams suggest possibilities, options, and radical renewals—assertions of human free will. In both we gain mastery over the world of matter, since it is still that world that we are reshaping—we see our own will dominate the sequence of events. The prisoner can always dream; and there is always the movies to go to when the daily grind gets too much. (Is it an accident that America defines itself by freedom, dreams, and movies?) If the central existential conflict of human life is between inexorable natural law and human spontaneity, then dreams and films are strikes in favor of the latter. They are human freedom made visible (as music is human freedom made audible). If only we could be star and director of our own life movie!

ABSORPTION

The dream holds the mind in a viselike grip, with no possibility of the mind wandering. While you are dreaming about swimming in mud, say, you cannot find yourself contemplating other things, such as what to do about the sagging gutter in your roof. But, of course, in real life you can easily be swimming in mud (well, water) and be thinking about your gutter problem: your mind can wander from what you are currently perceiving and you can still be perceiving it. Yet in dreams there is no room for this kind of inattentiveness—your attention is riveted to the content of the dream, even when it is relatively banal. Your mind is all there, in the moment, with nothing to distract it. So the dream has a unique hold over your attention, relentlessly sucking it in: it is attention dependent, in the sense that you cannot be having a dream you are not attending to—no attention, no dream.[16] Perhaps this is why dreams seem so vivid and overpowering, so utterly commandeering—they gobble up all the attention. That giant sucking sound you hear in your sleep is your dream drawing all the attention to itself. Because of this attention dependence, there cannot really be any periods during which the banality of the dream permits your attention to wander to more interesting topics. For it thus to wander, the dream itself would have to disappear. It isn't that dreams are just so fascinating in their content that you can't take your mind off them; it's rather that they cannot *exist* without the mind on them. Dreams have the power to erase everything from your mind but themselves.

Now I am not about to claim that movies possess *this* degree of power over the attention; clearly, your mind can wander from a movie that is not absorbing you and yet you are still seeing the movie. Nevertheless, I think it is fair to say that movies possess a remarkable power to engage the attention—more so, I suspect, than any other art form. When a movie is working, the viewer forgets everything else and becomes totally absorbed: there is now only the world of the movie, with all else erased from consciousness. Skillful direction manipulates the viewer's attention so that it is filled to the brim with the events on the screen: the close-up comes at just the right time; the music drives the point home;

the viewer is up there with the character on the screen. Viewer and character almost meld into one another. The habitually fretting and divided consciousness is unified and fully focused (and woe betide the talker in the next row!). Cinematic absorption is a phenomenon to be reckoned with. But how can those two-dimensional splashes of light, those flat ventriloquist's dummies, exercise such a powerful hold over human attention? The dream theory has a reply: because movie watching simulates dreaming, and dreaming is attention dependent. By entering a mental state that mimics dreaming, we engage the mechanisms of the dreaming mind, and among these is the capacity for intense absorption. Once the screen dream gains a hold, the attention is effectively hijacked. The attention can be distracted—say, by a loud noise—but the result is akin to waking up. While the movie is operating in the dream mode it is fully attended to. To put it differently, once the attention has been hooked, the dream impression becomes palpable. Full absorption in the movie becomes a potent source for generating the dream experience in the viewer. It is as if the mind is saying to itself: "If I'm this absorbed, it must be a dream I'm having." In any case, absorption and dreaming are inseparable, each reinforcing the other.

This brings us to the knotty subject of suggestibility and belief. In dreams we believe what we dream: if you dream you are about to be attacked by a bear, then you believe that this is so. It isn't that you have the sensory impression of being attacked by a bear but scoff at such an illusion; no, you really think it's about to happen—which is why you feel fear. It is a difficult question *why* you believe what you dream, but you clearly do, and the emotions are there to prove it.[17] One part of the answer appeals to suggestibility: you are abnormally suggestible during the dream, rather as you are under hypnosis. Your threshold for assent is drastically lowered. Anything your dream tells you, you believe, no questions asked. In the case of movies there seems to be a similar weakening of proper skepticism, at least for those who have not developed strongly critical minds (children mainly). The movie watcher seems abnormally suggestible, open to persuasion and propaganda—which is why movies have often been used to this end. It is comparatively easy to arouse the viewer's emotions and convictions. Again, if we ask why this is so, the dream theory has an answer: in simulating the dream state, the movie watcher enters a state of heightened suggestibility. This state is not as extreme as the dream state, but it approximates that state; thus beliefs are easily encouraged, opinions shaped. It is sometimes said that people these days get their basic beliefs from the movies; the dream theory tells us why: because the movie theatre is a place where people's suggestibility is abnormally high, owing to the dream mechanisms that are there evoked. Perhaps there should be a new category added to the ratings system: B, for "liable to lead to beliefs in unsuspecting viewers." Once you have someone in a dream state, just as a hypnotic state, you have him where you want him, belief-wise.

MEMORY

The recollection of dreams is notoriously poor. You may wake with a dream vividly before your mind, and the dream may be highly memorable in itself, but by lunchtime it is generally gone. It has been shown experimentally that the brain centers concerned with memory are relatively inactive during dreaming sleep. And yet dreams can themselves be repositories of unusually retentive memories: you can remember things in dreams that escape you altogether in waking life. Freud remarks on this in *The Interpretation of Dreams,* calling dreams "hyper-mnemonic"; forgotten scenes from childhood can, he observes, show up with remarkable fidelity within a dream.[18] So the dream has a good memory, even if we have a bad memory *for* the dream. What makes this especially curious is that poor retentiveness combines with strong impact: it is not as if the dreams we have make no impression on us—they often make a very powerful impression—but even so they generally leak quickly from memory (though, to be sure, there are dreams we remember our whole life). We are highly receptive to dreams, but not retentive of them. Dreams differ in this respect from ordinary waking experience, where impact and retention generally go together.

My memory of films is quite weak. I will often see a film I saw a few years ago and remember almost nothing of it (so I am not bored), and films slip quickly from my memory in a matter of days, if not hours. And this is not because I lack interest in them or that they make no impact on me; it's just that the impact is fleeting, and the memory fades rapidly. Although I know of no scientific studies of the question, my impression is that I am not alone in this—most people have a very porous memory when it comes to movies. You may remember the feelings a film evoked in you, and maybe the odd scene, but you will find it hard to remember the sequence of scenes in any detail (unless, of course, you watch it a number of times). People watching a movie they have seen before will state, "Ah, this is where such-and-such happens," and it turns out that they are quite wrong. Let us suppose that this is a fairly robust feature of human memory: why should it be so? If movies are psychologically akin to dreaming, then it is just what we might expect. Movies enter our minds as dreams do, but they also leave our minds that way too. There is a large impact, but a small residue. To confirm this anecdotal impression, one would have to do a serious study of both types of memory and compare them with other types of memory, of novels and of plays, say, as well as investigate whether people who are unusually good at remembering films are also good at remembering dreams. I am a mere philosopher, so I leave this task to more empirically inclined inquirers. But my prediction is that dream memory and film memory will turn out to be comparably feeble. Perhaps this is why people are often so keen to report on their dreams and the movies they have just seen: the impact was large, but without rehearsal the memory will quickly fade—so they bore you with their verbal rehashes.

TIMING

The point I am about to make, like some that follow, cannot be said to amount to much as a way of establishing the truth of the dream theory of film; but once that theory has acquired some traction (as, by now, I hope it has), it can serve to add to the circumstantial case in its favor. That is, once the theory has been accepted, at least as a good working hypothesis, certain facts slot nicely into place. So, astute reader, please don't accuse me of trying to *prove* the dream theory on the basis of flimsy evidence! With that caveat, then, consider the timing of movies. There are two aspects to this: when we watch them and how long they are. My optimal time for watching a movie is about eight or nine o'clock at night, and that seems a pretty popular time for many people. Now you might think this is just a matter of finding a convenient time between dinner and bedtime, but perhaps it has a more interesting explanation. Watching movies during the day is not my preference—nor do I like to nap during the day. After nightfall is really the best time for me. Now suppose the dream theory is true—isn't that what we would expect? We like to watch movies at the time when we would normally be dreaming—i.e., nighttime. But, you protest, that is false—most people don't go to bed that early! I don't; I go at around eleven or twelve: so am I not watching movies *earlier* than I am normally entering the sleep state? The timing, then, doesn't fit the theory. But, I reply, this is too hasty: it is true that in modern societies, with their electric lights and all-night diners, people stay up all hours, but not so long ago human beings were turning in pretty much when night fell, or soon after. People used to go to bed a lot earlier than we do now. Therefore, eight or nine at night would be the time at which they might already be enjoying a dreamy slumber. So the time at which I like to watch movies is actually the time at which, had I lived much earlier, I would have been dreaming. Interesting point, is it not? It is as if my ancient brain knows when it wants the dreaming to start, so it takes me to the movies just when I am forcing it to stay awake. As I say, let's not exaggerate the evidential power of this observation, but it is certainly consistent with the dream theory.

How long do people dream on an average night? The answer appears to be about two hours, in fits and starts. How long is the typical movie? It's also about two hours. But, you object, the movie is continuous while the dreaming is broken up. True, I respond, but remember that the continuity of a movie is qualified by the fact that it consists of a sequence of scenes, with some major lulls and changes of direction; and it used to be the case that people watched several films, short and long, in a single sitting, with breaks between them. So there is a kind of rough match between the duration of a movie experience and the duration of a night of dreams. Again, this is suggestive, if not probative. Once a movie exceeds the average duration of a night of dreaming, it becomes harder to watch, because the brain isn't designed to be in the dream state for so long. So directors, beware—don't try to stretch your viewers' allotment of dream time or they will wake up and want to leave.

TRANSITIONAL CONSCIOUSNESS

The transition from wakefulness to the dreaming state is not abrupt; there are intermediate stages. You lie down and start to nod off: this is when you may well experience so-called *hypnagogic images,* the kind of very vivid waking imagery that often precedes sleep. This period will usually be fairly brief, because sleep soon supervenes. Once you are asleep, there are two kinds of dreaming to contend with: REM and NREM sleep. REM sleep is the kind that accompanies deep dreaming, the kind with plots, themes, and personal reverberations. NREM sleep is accompanied by dreamlike states, often rehearsing experiences of the day, but it isn't the same as the full-blown REM dream state. The details don't matter for our purposes; what matters is that the mind passes through a succession of stages of imagery before it reaches the deep dreaming of REM sleep. The metaphor that suggests itself is that of the mind going *deeper* into its own inner dream resources. The process of entering the dream state is therefore gradual and graded; it is not a sudden descent into the dream mode.

But don't we find a parallel here with the typical movie experience? You enter the theatre, get comfortable, the lights go down, and what do you get? Not the main feature. You first have the trailers and maybe some ads; in the good old days there would be a newsreel or a cartoon or a short. Only when you have experienced some of this preliminary movie imagery are you expected to settle down for the main feature. You ease in. By the time the main feature starts, you are in full movie mode, ready to be swept away by what you are about to see. You are not expected to go abruptly from your local mall to the distant world of the movie, psychologically speaking; you need time to adjust, to put your consciousness in the mood. So hypnagogic imagery and NREM sleep are functionally analogous to trailers and newsreels, or whatever precedes the main film—they are devices of transition. Not only is watching the main film like having a dream; watching the preliminary stuff mimics the mental states that herald dreaming. In both cases, there is a period of transitional consciousness before deep immersion becomes possible. And there is something jarring about going into a movie theatre and having the main film come on immediately, as happens at press screenings of films; you need time to leave the waking world behind. Again, I intend this as a suggestive analogy, not as a cast-iron proof of the dream theory—it certainly fits with what I have already argued.

SPECIAL EFFECTS

In a way, all film consists of special effects. Artificial lighting is a special effect, if that means something not found in nature if left to its own devices. Any use of manmade scenery is a special effect. So is makeup. The very two-dimensionality of the screen, the creation of a world from projected light, the use of black-and-white—these are all special effects. Cinema *is* a special effect. What we normally think of these days as special effects—computer-generated images, tricks of motion, and distortions of the human form—are just developments of the very nature of film, which is a type of constructive artifice. Surely, much of our delight in viewing films involves an appreciation of these effects, even when the film is ostensibly "realistic." Any close-up of the human face, however natural, is really a special effect, since it does not replicate exactly anything we normally experience—no one's eyes are *that* big.

Where else do we find this kind of rampant artifice,

this augmentation of the real? Dreams, of course. Everything in a dream is a kind of heightening or transforming of what we experience in normal life; the real world comes to us filtered and distorted—surrealism at least had this right. Special effects involving motion are perhaps the most conspicuous—especially free flight, but also walking through solid objects, sudden shifts of location (like teletransportation), and marvels of speed and agility. People very often appear in elaborate disguises, as distorted versions of themselves, or with the appearance of someone else. It can get pretty weird in a dream. Things happen that don't, and can't, happen in reality. I remember when, at age eight, I saw the Wicked Witch of the East's legs shrivel under Dorothy's transplanted house, and felt a shiver of disgust and fear—it was just far too like the nasty things that happened in my nightmares. Dreams are a vast special effect, something unreal invented to pass itself off as reality.

But then, watching a movie will stir echoes of the dream world, by virtue of the distortions and trickery employed. The oddity of what we are seeing on the screen will resemble the oddity of the dream. Witnessing those cinematic special effects, the viewer's brain will recall its own special effects of the night. The fruitful fusion of film image and dream image will then ensue. The two sorts of image belong together, in contradistinction to the effects of nature, which by definition aren't special at all. If movies work by the twin principles of compression and amplification—packing a lot into a single image or sequence of images, and drawing attention to a significant detail by enlargement or other type of emphasis—then dreams too may be said to work this way, since they characteristically compress large, complex feelings into startlingly charged single images, and they often highlight a significant detail. I once had a dream of a woman whose entire physiognomy had been reduced to a pair of luscious red lips—a special effect that compressed a wealth of meaning into a single amplified detail. This dream image strikes me as intensely cinematic—as witness the many pairs of enormously enlarged painted lips we have all seen on the screen. That is what I mean by the special effects of compression and amplification, both forms of emotional emphasis.

SMELL

One view of cinema is that, ideally, it should approach as closely as possible the experience you would have if you were really confronted by the events depicted. Color improved on black-and-white, according to this view, because the real world is actually colored, so that color images approximate more closely the way things really are. The logical conclusion of this line of thought is that cinema should try to duplicate the experiences provided by the other senses, not just vision and hearing. Thus if I am seeing a man walk into a fetid swamp, I should be assailed by the olfactory experiences such a scene would afford—the screen should emit smells as well as sights and sounds. It might even attempt to produce tastes in the mouth, as the hero eats his heroic dinner. Yet movies have not in fact incorporated this feature; the movie theatre is an odor-free zone. Isn't this a failing in the "realism" movies purport to provide? Why hasn't smell entered the lexicon of movie techniques? Is it purely a technical matter—the difficulty of manufacturing smells for movie audiences to wrinkle their noses at?

Another view of cinema, the view I am adopting here, is that it approximates rather to the dream state. And it is an empirically well-established fact that dreams are not generally smelly: replete with visual and auditory images they certainly are, but olfactory imagery seems minimal to nonexistent. The olfactory parts of the brain seem not to be activated during dreaming; similarly for the gustatory parts. I may find myself in a fetid swamp in a dream, with animal noises all around, but I don't seem to have any smell images in my dream. I may *know* that something smells bad in my dream, but I don't have the image of this smell itself—though I certainly have visual images of the thing that smells. Dreams are a mix of visual and auditory images, but the other senses seem neglected. If so, movies are like dreams, and trying to endow them with dramatic odors will take them farther away from their true model. If smells reached our nostrils from the screen, we would lose the illusion of dreamlikeness, and the spell would be broken. So let's keep the movies odor-free.

OBJECT MEANING

When is an object more than an object? When it appears in a film. Film has the power to endow inanimate objects with a brooding inwardness, a life of their own. The early film theorist Siegfried Kracauer, in "The Establishment of Physical Existence," an essay about the world-revealing powers of the camera, writes as follows: "Actually, the urge to raise hats and chairs to the status of full-fledged actors has never completely atrophied [since the early days of cinema]. From the malicious escalators, the unruly Murphy beds, the mad automobiles in silent comedy to the cruiser *Potemkin,* the oil derrick in *Louisiana Story* and the dilapidated kitchen in *Umberto D.,* a long procession of unforgettable objects has passed across the screen—objects which stand out as protagonists and all but overshadow the rest of the cast."[19] And among these memorable objects I would add assorted shoes, swords, rings, keys, music boxes, lockets, guns, sleds, broomsticks, and houses. By means of the close-up and other modes of object salience, these items of hardware have been raised to the condition of sentience and will; at any rate, so our anthropomorphic minds have interpreted their screen presence. The object acquires a meaning, a symbolic weight—it becomes an active participant in the unfolding drama. If the screen elevates the actor to the status of spiritual body, then it also raises inanimate objects a notch in the ontological hierarchy, to the level of the animate. The light projected onto the screen operates somewhat like Frankenstein's bolts of lightning—it infuses life into the inanimate. The malevolent object is actually a stock character in movies—tidal waves, lava, fire, cars. Such objects appear to us as determined, volatile, cunning, ingenious, and relentless.

But it is equally true that in dreams objects often take on a charged existence. I recently had separate dreams in which a book and a shoe appeared carrying immense significance—the book as a repository of genius (Nabokov's *Lolita,* in the dream I mentioned earlier) and the shoe as a remnant of an absent friend. In both cases the objects were presented in astonishing detail, with a preternatural clarity, and they seemed to sum up a whole web of human relationships. I could fill a book with my dreams about cars and their wayward ways, their determination to thwart my efforts to get from A to B. We all have dreams about objects, familiar and unfamiliar, that play some sort of psychological role—that condense some psychic constellation into their coiled quiddity. The object seems to speak to us, to demand our attention; and yet it is still just an object (not like a cartoon character or a talking animal). Once again, then, we can discern a shared property of films and dreams, and perhaps we are psychologically prepared for the charged role of objects in films by the fact that this is a regular feature of our dream life. In both domains certain privileged objects are plucked from the usual clutter of stuff and implanted meaningfully into our minds—they come to inhabit that strange no-man's land between living consciousness and inert matter.

INTERPRETATION

Neither films nor dreams are inherently verbal—just think of the early days of silent films and of the dreams of animals and prelinguistic children. But linguistic practices have grown up around them: there is talk *in* films and dreams, and there is talk *about* films and dreams. As Wittgenstein would put it, there are "language games" of reporting our dream experiences and our film experiences. Dreams and films seem to lend themselves to this kind of follow-up chatter, even to demand it. We all know those individuals who insist on describing in great detail the movie they have just seen or the dream they just had—those people who are known in the technical scientific literature as movie or dream *bores.* They clearly feel a compulsion to verbalize what is not in itself verbal. And there are also those individuals who make their living engaging in such talk—movie critics and psychoanalysts (and theorists of film). There is clearly an appetite for commentary on dreams and films. Moreover, this commentary frequently takes the form of *interpretation:* the dream or movie presents itself as in need of deciphering in some way—the meaning seems obscure or hidden. We need not go the full Freudian hog with this in order to accept that dreams cry out for interpretation, even when the interpretation doesn't require any appeal to unconscious attitudes and feelings. Dreams and movies *symbolize* things, in some sense, and therefore need to be interpreted. A film may be really about the general question of racial inequality, say, even though it is explicitly only the story of one black man's invitation to dinner. A dream about forgetting my notes when about to give an important lecture might stand for my general anxiety about pontificating on philosophy. In both cases we have a primarily visual medium being translated into verbal discourse, where the verbal discourse tries to penetrate the meaning latent in the visual medium. We have an *analysis* of something that seems not to carry its full meaning on its face. Thus, in their need for interpretation, and in their propensity to be reported by their recipients, dreams and movies share a connection to language that is not inherent in them. More strongly, they appear to *seek* such a connection: there is an *urge to tell* in both cases. We want to be able to *understand* dreams and movies in verbal terms. Again, this underscores their psychological affinity. Maybe, indeed, the telling of movies is an offshoot of a prior urge to report our dreams.

STARS

I know I am not alone in sometimes dreaming of movie stars. I once had a dream in which I was explaining to some friends my lack of success in the dating game, and I sputtered out the words, "I'm not Brad Pitt, you know." At that moment I realized that Brad Pitt himself was seated opposite me at the table and looking a little miffed. I apologized to him for taking his name in vain, and he took it in good part. Similar dreams are often reported by people I've talked to. Why might this be? Because people have already seen the movie stars in the dreams they have on a Friday night at the multiplex. If a movie is like a dream, then the characters in movies are like the characters in dreams. I dreamed about Brad Pitt because he was already a fixture in my dream landscape; I'd dreamed about him many times before—while seated with my face upturned at a movie screen. The intimacy involved in admitting him to my dream world simply mirrors the intimacy he commands by appearing in my screen dreams (I will talk more in chapter 7 about celebrity and the dream theory). This mingling of dream and film, this migration of characters from one to the other, is predictable if films are experienced as dreamlike. My brain put Brad into my dream because he has already featured in the dream state of movie watching; it makes no firm distinction, recognizes no fixed boundary. In their "deep structure" movies and dreams traffic in the same basic forms. And yes, when we speak of a star as "dreamy" or a "dreamboat," we are latching onto something literally true. Of course, you are always the main star of your dreams—the lover, the action man, the moral crusader—but you are happy to play alongside the more public stars that feature in those communal dreams. My brain's dream producer gave Brad Pitt a cameo role in my dream, my night movie, because of his leading role in the light-projected kind I have seen so often. We dream of movie stars because they already carry the aura of the dream with them.

ACTIVE AND PASSIVE

Are we active or passive when we watch a film? Is the mind working or relaxing? We are both. We passively receive, through our sense organs, the images that populate the screen—simple seeing is a process of passive reception. But we also *interpret* what we see: we employ our imagination to construct the characters and story line, and this is an active business. This kind of imaginative seeing is an amalgam of active and passive, construction and reception. Similarly, when we dream we are simultaneously active and passive. We feel ourselves to be passive recipients of the experiences that crowd our consciousness, as if we are simply seeing things; but it is also true that the dream is an imaginative product—something actively put together. We are thus a passive audience of the dream and an active creator of it. I will leave it to the critic Bruce Kawin to derive the obvious conclusion, as explicitly as I could possibly wish:

> Watching a film and having a dream are both passive and active events. The dreamer/audience is physically cushioned in a darkened room, most of his movements restricted to slight shifts of position in a bed or chair, and mentally in various degrees of alertness, watching a visual process that often tells a story and often masks/presents some type of thought. In both cases the eyes move and the mind exercises creative attention. The dreamer might be considered more creative since the dream manifests his own thought processes, but the role of the film audience is also an active one since the viewer creates his own experience of the work . . . Although the dreamer is completely responsible for the dream, he usually avoids this awareness and casts himself in the role of participant or spectator; although the filmmakers are responsible for the movie, the viewer decides which film to attend and so chooses the general content of his experience. Thus dreamer and film-goer approach a middle ground of pseudo-responsibility for what is watched.[20]

This puts the point nicely, though I would prefer to emphasize the active role of the imagination in creating the movie we "watch"; for in a real sense the movie takes place inside our own head—the screen is merely the trigger for this inner activity. So in this subtle interweaving of passivity and activity, wherein the actively constructed presents the aspect of the passively received, we find the distinctive character of the two types of experience. We are authors of our dreams and of the movies we "watch," but we feel ourselves to be merely their passive audience. This curious hybrid state unites the movie experience with the dream experience in a unique and powerful way.

Five

REVIEWING THE DREAM THEORY

WAKING DREAMS

Having pointed out the many virtues of the dream theory of film experience, I now want to address some objections to this theory. The most obvious objection can be bluntly put as follows: watching a film can't be like being in a dream because you are *awake* while watching a film. Dreaming is a sleeping activity of the mind, but movie watching involves full waking consciousness of the world around you. How then can watching a movie be like being in a dream? Although it is certainly true that you are not asleep while watching a film, and that you are while having a dream, the relationship between wakefulness and dreaming is not as simple and clear-cut as the objection assumes. Remember, to begin with, those intermediate states of consciousness I mentioned in the previous chapter—hypnagogic imagery and NREM sleep. A person gradually enters the full sleep state, and gradually emerges from it. There are times at which it is simply not clear whether the person is awake or not—they are "half-awake" or "semiconscious." We are *more* or *less* unconscious. Our sleep can be *light* or *deep*. Perhaps what we call waking might just as well be described as extremely light sleep, as sleep might be seen as very diminished wakefulness (we are certainly very *alert* during REM dreaming sleep). It's not an all-or-nothing thing; it's more of a continuum. The movie watcher, then, might be described as entering a light sleep, an alteration of consciousness *approximating* sleep. And I think it is undeniable that the consciousness of the movie watcher is *trancelike.* You enter a state of being mesmerized. The movie exerts a hypnotic effect on you. Such states are in the same family as regular sleep. The experience of leaving the theatre often involves rubbing the eyes, stretching, blinking—generally acting as if you have just been roused from sleep. And there is that tuning out of everything except for the film, which happens mainly in the head anyway.

There is an even more telling point to be made: *the dreaming mind is not confined to the sleeping hours.* We often recall our dreams during the day, spontaneously or because we are reminded of them; we may then recycle the dream experience in our waking consciousness, savoring it or recoiling from it. When this occurs, the dream mechanisms are reactivated—the experience of the dream is rerun in attenuated form. So the content of a dream experience can occur in full consciousness, though as a remnant of an earlier dream. It is not that dreaming and waking are sealed compartments; one bleeds into the other. We dream about what we experience during waking hours, and we also sense the echoes of our dreams in our conscious hours. The dreaming mind has not totally shut down during the day. Also, unconscious dream work goes on during the day, so that the unconscious mind is active with dream concerns when the conscious mind is otherwise engaged. Movie watching is therefore accompanied by unconscious dream activity. It is oversimplified to suppose that the dreaming mind only wakes up, so to speak, during sleep.

But there is a yet more dramatic demonstration of the compatibility of dreaming and wakefulness: namely, insanity. Psychologists have often pointed to the kinship between insanity and the dreaming mind: the schizophrenic is locked in a permanent paranoid dream, and the dreamer is a temporary schizophrenic. J. Allan Hobson has given striking evidence that the dreaming mind is highly akin to the state of *delirium,* in his book *Dreaming as Delirium.*[1] It turns out that the chemical state of the brain is markedly similar in dreaming and delirium, which is not surprising in view of the evident psychological similarities—distorted reality sense, disorganized thought processes, hallucinatory images. But the mentally disturbed person is not, in any ordinary sense, *asleep,* so the dream process can be activated in a full-blooded fashion in conscious subjects. The dreaming mind can be fully active in people who are completely awake; the dream machinery is whirring away, though not in a state of conventional sleep. There is thus no logical bar to supposing that movie watchers have their dream minds brought into operation. It isn't, of course, that movie watching is a form of insanity (but then there are those "movie nuts" . . .); it is just that the case of insanity shows that wakefulness and dreaming are not mutually exclusive. The dreaming mechanisms can be activated in different ways, to different degrees, in different circumstances, while the rest of the mind is doing whatever may be called for. There is no simple dichotomy between sleeping and dreaming, on the one hand, and not sleeping and not dreaming, on the other. We might say, being cautious, that in movie watching the dreaming mind is *partially* activated, meaning that the whole panoply of the typical dream state is not in play. Or we could say that movie watching is a *hybrid* state, mixing dream elements and waking elements. In any case, there is no commitment on the part of the dream theory to the dubious claim that movie watching is a type of sleeping.

A few words about daydreams are in order. The occurrence of daydreams is further evidence that the dreaming mind is not active only during sleep, since it is very plausible to suppose that the mechanisms in the brain that allow daydreams to be generated are the same as those that manufacture night dreams, or at least there is an overlap. A powerful reverie, perhaps under the influence of a stimulant or a fever, surely resembles dreaming in many ways—the dreaming mind on its day shift, as it were. Clearly, daydreams occur during our waking hours, so again the dream mechanisms can do their thing in the glare of daylight, though in a modified form.

But this raises the question of why I don't compare movie watching to daydreams instead of night dreams. Well, there are some similarities, as we would expect given that the two types of dreaming are themselves similar, but there are also important dissimilarities. The main one is that daydreams are driven by the conscious will of the daydreamer—*she* is in control of what she daydreams. You can decide what to have a daydream about, and you can decide when to end it; what goes in your daydream is pretty much what you choose.

Thus the agency behind the daydream is experienced by the daydreamer as coming from inside. But the agency behind both night dream and movie is experienced as coming from *outside:* it is important to both that they be experienced passively, as not coming from the viewer's own will. Only this will allow for the kind of *surprise* that can accompany both dreaming and movie watching—things happen that you can't predict. But your daydreams predictably play out what you decide to put in them (consider a typical sexual fantasy): this can be gratifying, but it lacks somewhat in the suspense department. Movies specialize in suspense, so they are decidedly *not* like daydreams. You don't control what comes up on the movie screen, as you do on your inner daydreaming screen.

Secondly, daydreams are simply not as *vivid* as dreams. Except in pathological cases, daydreams do not overpower, unman, shatter; but dreams can do all this and more. The power of film thus needs a more robust analogue than the thin and paltry image of the daydream—something with more heft and thud. The night dream can dominate consciousness in a way no daydream can, and its individual images attain a degree of clarity and clout that daytime images cannot match; this is what we need to capture the charged intensity of the movie image. The daydream is more like a shadow-puppet show, performed with your own hands, instead of a tidal wave of heightened reality coming right between your eyes.

YOU YOURSELF

It may now be objected that there is a crucial disanalogy between film and dream—namely, that dreams are always about you, the dreamer, while movies are never about you (unless you are the kind of person to have films made about you). You always crop up in your dreams like a bad penny, but unless you are a screen actor you don't crop up in the movies you watch. Again, this is quite true—but the situation is a little subtler than the objection allows. Self-centeredness is a very peculiar property of dreams: is it a mark of our habitual human egocentricity, or does it reflect some deep truth about the very structure of dreaming? For it is not that you *mostly* dream about yourself, as you may mostly *talk* about yourself; it is not that you regularly put yourself at the center of your dreams, but occasionally let someone else take the lead role. So this is not common or garden-variety selfishness, as if you have an overweening desire to hog the dream limelight. It is rather that you *can't* dream about anyone else—you *necessarily* put yourself at the center. Why? Isn't it at least logically possible that you might have a dream in which you are mercifully absent? Why can't you dream about your friends and family having an adventure, with you not even in the picture? (You could certainly write a story like that.) The dream scripts seem to be inexorably drawn toward the dreamer; yet it is hard to see why this should be a rigid necessity. What is it about dreaming consciousness that *forces* such egocentricity on dreams? Take the least self-centered person in the world, totally self-effacing, never talks or even seems to think about himself—he *still* dreams exclusively and obsessively about himself every night for hours! This ought to strike us as puzzling, and I admit I have no good explanation for it—it has perplexed me for a long time. One interesting aspect of the question is that it does at least raise the conceptual possibility of dreams that are not self-centered, so that films might approximate this logically conceivable type of dream (though not the dreams regular folks have). But this is less than satisfactory from my point of view, because I want movies to resemble the dreams that humans *actually* have, not the kind they might have in some possible world in which they dream less egocentrically. So what should we say of the disanalogy that obtains between dreams as we actually have them and films?

I think the objection can be turned on its head: the egocentricity of dreams *helps* in generating a certain attitude that defines our relationship to the screen. I mean the attitude of *identification.* There are two sorts of identification to consider: identification with the camera and identification with a character on the screen. The camera views the action from a specific position, its own movements affecting what appears on the screen. We naturally identify with the camera, so that we are brought into visual relation to the action: if it is two feet from the heroine's face, then it is *as if* we are; if it moves, it is *as if* we are moving too. Our own eye is identified with the eye and angle of the camera, so that we are placed inside the action through this identification—we certainly don't experience the action as if we were looking at it from the *other* side! But it is the second sort of identification that really bears the imprint of the dream: you may not be literally up on the screen yourself, but you *identify* with the people who are. This identification may be monogamous or promiscuous: you may pick a single character and stick with him throughout the film, typically the designated hero; or you may shift your allegiance back and forth, now choosing this person, now that. Whatever you do, there is always *someone* on the screen whose place you are imaginatively occupying; and without this your involvement would be greatly diminished. You are forever putting yourself in a screen character's shoes, empathizing with him, feeling his pain. Often, though not always, this is because you feel you have been in something like his predicament, so that you can easily imagine what it must be like to be him. When I watch *Brief Encounter* (probably my favorite film), I feel a strong sense of identification with the female lead, Laura, played by Celia Johnson, and less with the male lead, Alec, played by Trevor Howard—probably because I feel a stronger resemblance of personality between Laura and myself. In any case, there is no doubt that I feel myself to be up there on the screen, right with her. People often report that they feel a particular film to be "about me"—about their own lives.

So the self is not so absent from the movies as may initially appear. And I conjecture that the prevalence of the self in dreams aids this process of identification: we are just so *used* to finding ourselves the center of the action in our dreams that we readily insert ourselves into those celluloid dreams. Given that movies resemble dreams in other ways, we naturally locate ourselves in the stories being told—we bring them even closer to the dream by the mechanism of identification. So it is not required that the films you see be *literally* about you in order that the structure of your relationship to them duplicate that of the dream; it is enough that they *approximate* this structure—and identification permits this.

WHAT WE SEE

We see the images on the screen, but while dreaming we don't *see* anything—our eyes are closed, and we are fast asleep. The film is literally an object of vision, but the dream is at best an object of the *mind's* eye. So aren't they importantly different? Again, there is truth to this, but it is oversimplified. First, as I have noted, the movie that we "see" is largely a product of our imagination. The images we literally see are splashes of light that act as stimuli to our constructive mental processes: we don't see the characters and scenes at all—we imagine them. So movie watching is heavily imaginative, just as dreaming is. Yet it is still true that we see the images on the screen, even if the characters and story line are accessed by the imagination. But again, matters are blurrier than we might suppose, because we also perceive sensory stimuli during dreaming sleep, and these stimuli can find their way into our imaginative constructions as we dream. Thus consider the well-known example of the alarm clock and the wedding bells: the sound from the clock enters the dreamer's ears and as a result he experiences wedding bells in the dream he is having. He has interpreted the alarm clock in a certain way and incorporated the sound in the story line of his ongoing dream. This kind of thing happens all the time, and indeed it was once believed that *all* dream images result from perceived stimuli being incorporated into the dream. But then, dreams *can* result from the perception of stimuli in the environment, as a hand passing over the eyelids may be experienced within the dream as a plane overhead. It is in fact possible to manipulate a person's dreams by such means. In principle, I daresay, one could control the entire course of someone's dream by deft choice of external stimuli, though how the dreamer interprets such stimuli will be up to her. So there is no incompatibility between seeing and hearing, on the one hand, and dreaming, on the other—indeed, the very things seen and heard may play a constructive role in generating dream content.

But isn't this, structurally, just like the movie case? The images on the screen are put there to manipulate the viewer's imagination, so that perceiving and imagining can mix in a fruitful act of mental construction. Suppose we developed a technology for dream manipulation that bombarded the sleeper with stimuli in such a way that we could determine the course of the dream (at least up to the point at which the sleeper's interpretative processes intervened): wouldn't this be essentially like what we now do with movie stimuli? Certainly, the fact that the dream is thus controlled has no tendency to show that the subject is not dreaming! Dreams, as I said, can be produced by outside stimuli reaching the dreamer's senses. So there isn't the sharp distinction between dreaming and movie watching that the present objection presupposes. Watching a movie is like dreaming about the stimuli that reach us from the screen. It's all alarm clocks and wedding bells.

DREAMS AND ART

Dreams are not art and movies are. Dreams are *artifice*—human constructs made with the imagination—but dreams are shapeless, chaotic, meaningless, *inartistic.* Now it is tempting to reply that a great many films aren't art, either. But this is too easy a reply, since even the most artistically challenged film has a kind of structure and shape that dreams sorely lack, and the most coherent and meaningful dream can't compete with a serious dramatic film for artistic accomplishment. It makes, indeed, little sense to try to evaluate dreams aesthetically: we don't have dream critics the way we have movie critics. Dreams can contain some striking visual effects, but watching a serious filmic work of art doesn't seem much like the regular run-of-the-mill dream from an aesthetic point of view. Are we to say, then, that only the least artistic films are really dreamlike? Is it that when confronted by a decent film, the brain says: "I thought this was going to be a dream, but it's far too artistic for that, so it can't be"? That would be a major concession on the part of the dream theory, a big letdown.

However, even if we took that line, there would still be all the other resemblances I have cited, so the analogy would not be totally hobbled. But I think we can say something stronger, and more interesting: a movie is a dream *idealized.* A movie is a dream *as we wish we had them.* It would be nice if our dreams could be finer things, stories worth putting on paper and selling to Hollywood. It would be wonderful to wake up in the morning with recollections of Shakespeare-quality (or even Spielberg-quality) dreams. Our dreams are just not that entertaining, and they stink in the retelling. A dream may supply an *idea* for a film, but it will require a lot of reworking before anyone will green-light it.

In short, movies *improve* on dreams; a movie is a dream that has been artistically shaped and edited. What we experience in the movie theatre, then, is not the rough cut of a typical dream, but a dream as it has been rendered into art. Accordingly, part of what we are responding to, and appreciating, is the elevation of the dream to a higher level. We perceive the dreamlike quality of the film—as indicated by the other markers I have enumerated—and in addition we sense the improvement on the homegrown product. It is like a dream, *only better.* We get to have a dream, with all its power and pizzazz, and as a bonus we are treated to a superior version of dreaming. What could be better? Film is not the dream unfiltered, neat, but the dream as it is *in our dreams*—films are the dreams we dream of having. If only they could be inserted straight into our brains, so that they could take over from the usual crappy dreams we have! If only the dream studio in our heads could be taken over by a really crack producer! The appeal of movies, then, partly involves their transcendence of their roots—their ability to transmute and advance the dream materials that essentially compose them. The history of film, accordingly, is the steady improvement of projected dreams (though some early films are artistically as accomplished as anything we see today). I had a dream, only last night, of surfing a wave, and I can see the glassy curvature in my mind's eye now; but I know very well that the latest surf movie will greatly improve on the experience for me—there will be a story, bigger waves, more of them, and so on. A film is really a dream as it aspires to be.

PUBLIC AND PRIVATE

Films are seen seated in a public place; dreams are had at home, in private, usually in a bed. Movie watching is communal; dreaming is solitary. Is this an objection to the dream theory? No, because these differences are entirely contingent, and superficial. Obviously, there is nothing to prevent you, in principle, from watching a movie alone, and the experience is not *essentially* different, somehow less "cinematic." I often go to the movies alone in the afternoon, when there is hardly anyone else there, and yet I don't feel that I haven't really seen a movie. Equally, communal dreaming is a possibility: you could get together with other people in a big room and go off to sleep; and there is no logical bar to having the same dream they do. As for sleeping in a bed, you can dream while seated and watch a movie while lying flat.

BELIEF

In a dream you are not aware that you are dreaming, while in the movies you are aware that you are watching a movie.

A corollary of this is that you believe what you dream, but you don't believe what you see on the screen. There is a difference in the reflective knowledge possessed in the two cases. In the one case there is a confusion of the dream world with the real world, while in the other there is no confusion of the screened world with the real. What should we say to this?

First, never underestimate the power of absorption. Particularly with children, but also with adults, there can be deep immersion in what appears on the screen, so that the rest of the world is forgotten, and no thought of being in a movie theatre spoils the flow of the film into the viewer's consciousness. He or she is *there.* This state—trancelike, fixated, and flooded—approximates the absorption characteristic of the dream. This is when the flinching at danger, the empathetic tears, the racing heart all come into play; the mind has departed its place in the movie theatre and entered the world of the film. Absorption is a matter of degree, and movie absorption is on a scale at the other end of which is the deep absorption of the dream. There is no sharp dichotomy here.

Secondly, we must not neglect the phenomenon of the *lucid dream.* This is the dream in which its status *as* dream is transparent to the dreamer (it may also permit the dreamer to control the course of the dream by conscious will). Such dreams are rare for most people, but in some they are common. It is as if the dream comes stamped with a sign that reads: "This Is Only a Dream." Naturally, belief is not secured in such a dream state: if you know it is just a dream, you don't go around believing it. You may allow yourself to become absorbed in the fiction, but all along you are aware that that is what it is. This is very like the normal state of semiabsorption that accompanies adult immersion in a film: you may become absorbed in the story, but lurking in the margins of awareness is the knowledge that you are really in a movie theatre. The fiction is tagged as such in your consciousness of it. So the precise analogue to this kind of movie watching is the lucid dream. The ordinary dream may lack the kind of reflective understanding commonly found in the movies, but lucid dreaming restores the analogy. So, to be very precise, we might say that movies most resemble lucid dreams—but they are dreams, nonetheless.

THE SCREEN

Movies are seen on a screen, and dreams are not: isn't that a disanalogy? Well, movies cost money to see, and dreams do not—that doesn't cut very deep. To be sure, I earlier rejected the notion of a mental screen on which our dreams are projected—there is no such screen. But the screen of the movie theatre is really a *vanishing* screen: you don't see the screen once the movie has started, as I pointed out in chapter 2. The screen is not part of your subjective experience; it is merely part of the actually existing apparatus. The presence of the screen is entirely virtual—more of an absence, really. The screen does not act to negate the dreamlike impression created by the movie, because it is simply too recessive, too ancillary. If there were no solid screen, but just empty air magically producing the image, it would make no real difference to the movie-watching experience. The screen is no more vital to the experience than the curtain in front of it is.

DREAMLIKENESS

I hear a voice protesting from the back row: "You say that movies are like dreams, but movies sure don't *seem* like dreams—you don't find yourself thinking 'Golly, this is so dreamlike' as you watch a movie. In fact, the only time you ever think something like that is when the film includes a dream sequence—you know, with hazy lights and echoing voices. The rest of the time movies seem totally, um, realistic." If I am not mistaken, I have already answered this objection in the last chapter: *dreams* don't seem dreamlike, either. We have two perspectives on dreams, from the inside and from the outside. From the outside, in retrospect, dreams strike us as dreamlike, not easily confusable with real events; their bizarreness and lack of consonance with the rest of our experience is evident. But from the inside, while we are having them, they don't strike us as dreamlike at all (unless we are having a lucid dream); they strike us as totally, um, realistic. So it is essential for films to *be* dreamlike that they not *seem* dreamlike. Doses of surrealism subvert this condition, which is why surrealism is misleading about the nature of dream experience—surrealist works capture only the outside perspective. Ordinariness is the essential characteristic of the inside perspective—as if this could happen to anyone at any time.

COMEDY

Comedy provides an interesting challenge. Do we have humorous dreams? If not, there is one genre of film that has no dream counterpart, so that watching a comedy at least isn't dreamlike. Now it is true, I think, that we do not experience laughter in our dreams: that is, we don't find ourselves with the attitude of amusement in mid-dream. Dreams are a solemn and serious affair. Some people I have talked to dispute this, maintaining that they do have comedy dreams; but upon closer examination they always seem to mean that they dream about funny things—which is not the same thing. It is quite true that funny things occur in dreams, and people often derive a lot of amusement recounting their dreams for others (the others are often somewhat less amused). But, again, this is an outside view of the dream, not an inside view. If I dream of turning into a tortoise and finding it hard to get across the road before a car hits me, I may have dreamed something hilariously funny in the telling, but you can be sure it didn't feel too funny as I was dreaming it. So I doubt that dream amusement occurs, at least in anything like the form it takes while we are awake (in contrast, fear and elation *do* occur in dreams). But then, I have a bit of a theoretical problem: comedy films aren't like any dream state we are accustomed to, so they seem like a counterexample to the theory.

I think the reply to this is that for comedy films to be like dreams, dreams don't need to have amusement occurring *within* them. What they need is for the kinds of things that comedy films *contain* to occur within them. After all, in all the best comedies nobody is laughing *in the film*—the characters don't know they are in a comedy. They are behaving with perfect seriousness; it is we, the members of the audience, who find the whole thing enormously amusing. Take *Dr. Strangelove:* everybody in this film takes himself and his actions incredibly seriously—the film, after all, is about the nuclear threat. But we viewers are convulsed at their very solemnity and the bitter comedy of their bluster. In the same way, a dream can be funny without anyone within it ever cracking a smile— in particular, without the dreamer himself experiencing any amusement. Thus people will say, "I had a really funny dream last night—do you want to hear it?," even when they report on how terrified they felt within the dream. So, yes, there are comedy dreams, after all, just as there are comedy films; but this doesn't require that the dreamer be amused inside the dream, as opposed to later. We all have our Charlie Chaplin dreams, in which we have big shoes, no home, and a peculiar walk, but we don't find these very amusing in the having of them. Also, of course, we may dream that someone is laughing, perhaps at our expense; but that doesn't mean that the emotion of amusement is being felt in the consciousness of the dreamer. When I am amused at the cinema, then, it is like my amusement at the recollection of a dream, not like my amusement from inside the dream, which is nonexistent. Still, it is a peculiar fact that the emotion of amusement doesn't seem to occur within dreams, though other emotions do.

THE MEDIUM

The final objection I want to consider is that the dream theory cannot be the whole story: there must be more to the movie experience than the analogy with dreams suggests, for we need to recognize the contribution made to the experience by the film medium itself. We need to make room for our visual relationship to the screen and the way the images on it affect our consciousness. The screen image has certain formal properties, to which we are perceptually related, and these properties will carry a meaning for the viewer in virtue of their intrinsic nature. The dream theory omits mention of these formal properties and their significance, so it cannot be a complete theory of the movie experience. For example, film images are two-dimensional and composed of light—how does this empirical fact fall within the dream theory? Nothing in my head is flat and composed of light when I dream!

I agree entirely with this point: the dream theory is not a complete theory. But it was never meant to be; it is just one part of an overall theory, which needs to take into account our visual relationship to the screen and the metaphysical meaning of the movie image. Obviously, we need something in order to be able to *distinguish* dreams from films—something that separates them, since they are clearly not the same thing. The point of the dream theory is just to insist that dreams and films are deeply united despite their formal differences. The dream theory captures a *component* of the movie experience, not its entire nature; for that we need to investigate also our perceptual and cognitive relation to the screen image. Summing up, somewhat crudely, we can say that movie watching involves looking *into* the screen image, finding there the dematerialized body, and undergoing an experience with many of the features of dreams. The total experience is an amalgam of these three elements.

Six

HOW TO MAKE A DREAM

PRODUCTION

Heretofore, the topic has been how we experience films and dreams once they have come into existence. In this chapter I shall switch attention to film and dream *production*—how films and dreams arrive in the world, what the gestation process is. We know quite a bit about film production—what the basic processes and components are—and I think these can shed light on what must lie behind the production of dreams. Dreams, in other words, are created in ways significantly analogous to the production of movies. Dream production can be illuminatingly compared to film production.

Let me start from our normal, naive view of how dreams come into being. We suppose, I think, that they arise spontaneously, with little preparation, more or less at the time they are "viewed." We assume that the brain manufactures them with minimal effort and in short order; they just "pop into our heads" as we sleep. All we consciously experience of dreams is the end product; whatever lies behind their production is hidden from conscious view. We therefore tend to suppose that nothing much *is* hidden—what we see is what there is. Compare ordinary visual perception: all we experience of this process is the end product, the conscious percept that occurs in our mind as a result of the brain's processing of incoming stimuli. At the most naive level we tend to think that the external object just makes its way into the mind, that it meets consciousness without any intermediate processing—rather as if consciousness were a box into which the object is placed. Certainly, our percepts arise without any conscious effort, apparently spontaneously, just as if the process were a simple matter of the object imprinting itself on the sensorium—a primitive stamping operation. But, of course, this naive view is just that: the visual process is far more complex than the deliverances of introspection suggest. First, the object itself does not strike the eye at all; it emits light rays that enter the eyeball and impinge on the retina. The image formed on the retina, which is fragmentary and two-dimensional, then stimulates the optic nerve, and an elaborate process of interpretation is set in motion, eventuating in a conscious visual percept. Vision scientists have studied this process, noting how complex the transformations of the retinal image must be, and how multiple the computations that lead to the final percept—which then gives the misleading impression of having just popped into consciousness from nowhere. The causal background to even the simplest percept is immensely complex and multilayered—this much is now accepted fact.[1] No one has any idea how to build a machine that can generate percepts in the way brains can—full-blown 3-D percepts from 2-D patterns of light striking the retina. In a way, this is a miraculous act of creation, not something like taking a fingerprint.

It is easy to draw people's attention to the elementary

facts of visual perception, because the eye is out there to be observed and people know what the retina is. It is clear enough that the visual system must go from a mere spot of electromagnetic energy on the retina to a rich conscious awareness of the external world. A sense of wonder at this process is therefore readily produced. But in the case of dream production the underlying apparatus is not out there for all to see; it is hidden in the recesses of the brain. The case for complexity must therefore be circumstantial. The best way to get a sense of this complexity is to compare what comes in through the senses with what comes out in the form of dreams—the input and output of the dream-production process. Dreams are, in some sense, based on sensory experience: the images they present are rooted in perception, and we dream about people and things that have been retained in memory from our perceptual encounters with them. When you have an image of a red truck, say, in your dream, this originated in experiences of red objects in the perceptible world, and dreams tend to be about familiar objects and situations. The input, then, consists of our ordinary perceptual experience. *But the output far exceeds the input.* Consider a dream I had only recently, which is still fresh in my mind; it is entirely typical of dreams generally, not especially ingenious or remarkable. I was back at my old Oxford college, in the senior common room chatting to some colleagues, just before dinner was due to start. Everyone was drinking—some drinking wine, some martinis, some whiskey. I couldn't manage to secure a drink for myself as I watched everyone else happily imbibing, and particularly coveted a martini I saw someone sipping. Finally, I managed to get hold of a carafe of wine, but all the glasses I could see had been used already, and I was embarrassed to be seen drinking out of someone else's glass—I must have examined fifty glasses of every conceivable shape and size, looking for a clean one. In the end I picked up a dirty glass, poured wine into it, and took a gulp—but it was some sort of strange cherry water, not wine at all. Disappointment. Everyone was now filing out to dinner, giving me funny looks. Then I realized I was wearing a scruffy sweatshirt, absurd striped pants, and a pair of muddy Wellington boots—to high-table dinner! I sought out the bathroom, hoping to make myself more presentable. As I entered the bathroom I saw that it had changed from the old days, being cavernous, full of fancy sculptures, and very expensively appointed—and yet absolutely filthy (I will spare you the details of what I saw in the toilet bowl). My eyes dwelling heavily on the besmirched porcelain of this fallen bathroom, I felt soiled myself.

Now let us not trouble ourselves with hidden meanings and Freudian speculations; what I want to point out is how unprecedented all this was in my own sensory history. Every sight in the dream was fresh, newly minted: I have never owned a pair of pants like that (nor would I!); I have never been in a bathroom full of sculptures; that cherry drink was like nothing I've ever experienced. It was all a product of my brain's inner creative powers (and I have mentioned only a portion of the full content of the dream). In no way could we think of this dream as some sort of simple transcription from experience, a mere imprint of waking perception; it was a radical transformation of my old experiences at Corpus Christi College—which, by the way,

I haven't visited in over ten years. I hadn't been thinking about Oxford recently, either—this dream just came "from the blue." What must strike us, then, is the yawning chasm between input and output—between my waking experience and the dream content. Somehow the brain must cross this gap, delivering the end product from the initial materials. That is, the brain must be capable of remarkable creative feats in producing a dream like this. Nor could I, at will, consciously generate the same experiences in the form of a daydream—the detail, vividness, and sense of reality would not be there. The pants alone, with their lurid stripes, their air of effete dishevelment, were a masterpiece of artistic production—perfectly designed to humiliate their unfortunate wearer, the very zenith of sartorial inappropriateness. Whoever dressed me in those pants knew what he was doing. And I've never *seen* a martini looking as inviting as the one being poured just out of my reach for some gray-bearded professor or other.

The first point to be made, then, is that dream production must involve some very elaborate processes of image and scene construction. Clearly, the intention of the dream was to make me feel frustrated and embarrassed—this was its emotional crux—and the sensory contents (the awful pants, the inviting drink) were designed to bring this about. Thus the dream has a means-end structure—an emotional end and a sensory means. It exhibits intelligent design. The interweaving of the sensory and emotional (discussed in chapter 4) aids this design. The dream-production process is creative, purposeful, and resourceful. How should we conceptualize this process? What kinds of stages might it involve? How might it be analyzed?

FILMMAKING

Here is where I want to invoke the analogy with film. Film production can be broken down, roughly speaking, into the following stages: concept, script, green-lighting, casting, design, sets, filming, editing, and distribution. This division is not intended as definitive or uniquely correct; further subdivisions might be made, and I haven't said anything about raising the money or paying the actors and crew, not to mention catering and so on. The stages I have listed are basic to the process. Someone has to have an idea of what he wants to make a film about; someone has to put together a written script, more or less complete; someone has to agree to make the film, to put resources into it; the film has to be cast; design, sets, and makeup must be arranged; the actual filming must take place, the movie being stored on a medium that can later be activated; the editor must step in to shape the film; finally, the film must be distributed and viewed. The entire process can take months or years and is obviously very complex, requiring the interplay of many separate agencies. A naive viewer, such as a child, might suppose that the action just happened before the camera spontaneously, that it just sprang into being somehow (after all, many movie watchers don't even know what a director or producer is, and some confuse actors with characters). A film, however, is an elaborate artifact, a product of intelligent design; what eventually appears on the screen is just the end product of a complex process of construction. My question, then, is whether this constructive process can be usefully compared to the process of dream construction.

I can only speculate here, since we know so little about how dreams are made, but I want to suggest that the film model provides a useful way to think about dream production. Let us then think of the dream machinery as a kind of team of separate agencies, each assigned its own job. The ideas man starts the process: he wants to make a dream revolving around a certain theme—say, my embarrassment at an academic gathering. Why the hell he would want to do that we don't know; we really don't understand why the brain generates dreams and why it generates the particular types of dreams it does. But it does, and the dreams seem to have recurrent themes—notably, anxiety and wish fulfillment. Perhaps the ideas man knows I am sensitive about this type of thing and wants to torment me; or maybe he thinks it will be good therapy to let me get these feelings out. In any case, emotions seem to be the primary source of dream ideas. But an emotion without a script is pretty pointless, so some sort of narrative has to be constructed to express the emotion. Thus the concept is turned into a script, a specification of what the dream will contain. But converting the script into an actual dream uses brain resources, and other ideas and scripts are competing for attention (since I have many emotions that are seeking some sort of dream outlet). So some scripts might languish in the offices of the dream team as others are given a robustly sensory form. Suppose, though, that a particular script strikes the executives in the dream hierarchy as ready to be made, that the time is ripe for a dream like this. Perhaps the dreamer has been preoccupied with a certain emotion lately, or she has neglected a certain emotion. Then the script might be green-lighted, slated for production. Thus the script about me in an Oxford senior common room was green-lighted for production, with other competing scripts turned down or held in abeyance.

The casting must begin (or maybe casting preceded green-lighting, if particularly colorful characters have already been penciled in). In the case of my dream, my twenty-four-year-old son, Bruno, was also with me (though I didn't mention this earlier); the gray-bearded professor had an especially smug and irritating look; and the bathroom attendant was a man who seemed both officious and downtrodden—his face spoke volumes. Each of these figures had a specific sensory form, a particular aura. One of the other members of the college present was someone I remember from the old days, not an invented character, and I recall him now as a little strict about college decorum. So each of these figures had to be selected to play a role described in the script—to give that role sensory presence. Then there is the matter of set design: everyone else seemed sensibly dressed (nice white jacket for the bathroom attendant), but clearly the scene won't work unless I am clad suitably outrageously—hence the wretched pants and Wellington boots. The director of the dream tells the wardrobe people to get something really horrible for me to wear, and they come up with tight striped pants from 1960s Carnaby Street. These matters having been settled, the dream can now be shot, with all the elements brought together. In other words, a record is laid down of how the dream images are to be sequenced when the dream occurs. But notice that this isn't the same as *show-*

ing the dream. That is a matter for further deliberation, a question of timing and rival projects. Finally, a date is selected, the dream screened, and I wake up having had the dream I have been reporting.

TIME LAG

The last phase of the dream-production process requires further comment. As I described it, there was a delay between filming and distribution—between making the dream and showing it. Why did I introduce such a delay? Why isn't the dream shown *while* it is being shot? Indeed, why do I assume that the whole process is temporally extended? Couldn't everything from concept to distribution happen at the same moment? The model I am working with is that the brain contains a library of potential dreams, waiting to be shown on a given night, instead of dreams being projected off the cuff each night. But why do I think of the matter this way? The answer is twofold. First, the process is just too complex to be accomplished on the fly: the dream content is too intelligent and cunning to be brought about instantly. It would take me a while to consciously think up the dream I described; it is hard to believe that the dream work itself could proceed in a sudden leap forward. That dream took planning, and malice aforethought. Maybe it had been in the process of construction over a number of years, with many a tweak and twist to get it just right. There is really no reason to believe that the entire creative process behind the dream took place on the night of the dream, the moment before the dream entered my dreaming consciousness; it is more plausible to suppose that it was spread out over time, perhaps going back as far as my days in Oxford (certainly the images of Oxford seemed remarkably fresh). That dream had been in the works for a while.

Secondly, the fact that dreams are so often rooted in the past suggests that they have been knocking around in our heads for some time. My dream about Oxford seemed like a *remnant* from the past, not just *about* the past. And why should my brain have created such a dream only just before its recent occurrence? Doesn't it make more sense to suppose that it created the dream at a time closer to the time of the experience being referred to? In fact, doesn't it make sense to suppose that the brain is continually creating dreams in response to the experiences of waking life? It takes an experience in, toys with it, tries out various dream scenarios, and maybe lays down a track for later use—all this happening unconsciously. The dream work is accordingly going on all the time, day and night, not just at the very time of dreaming. Dreams are a reworking of experience, so it makes sense to suppose that they are reworking it all the time. When a dream refers to the past, then, it is likely that at least some of the initial dream work was done at or around the time referred to. Some dream themes relating to Oxford may have been laid down in my unconscious years ago when I was still there; only now do they emerge into the light of night in the form of a conscious dream. As with film production, there is a considerable time lag between the early stages of production and the final viewing.

A further piece of evidence for the hypothesis of time lag

comes from empirical findings about the relation between the time of an experience and the time of dreaming about it. J. Allan Hobson reports that the optimal time lag here is about six or seven days: it takes that long for a dream to be constructed that refers to an earlier waking experience (not the day before, as some had claimed).[2] This suggests that the process *requires* such a time period: that's how long the brain *needs* to put together a decent dream. But we often dream of experiences that go back much farther, so presumably the dream work was initiated long ago. Thus our brains house a library of potential dreams, some still in production, not quite complete, and on a given night a decision has to be made about which dreams are going to take up valuable screening time. It is not that each night the brain enters the sleeping state and has *no idea* what dreams it will generate that night, hoping for inspiration as REM time approaches. No, it dips into its back catalogue. There is a scheduling of the dream calendar, with particular dreams tagged for release on given dates. The reasons for this timing are often obscure, though sometimes it is quite obvious why now is the time you are dreaming about such-and-such (as when you dream about an exam the day before you take one). However, it seems to me fantastically unlikely that dreams are cooked up on the spur of the moment, just when they are about to be unveiled, as if the dream machinery were idle for the rest of the time. It is far more plausible to suppose that dream creation is an ongoing activity, as much in the day as in the night. The unconscious is hard at work on its dream projects for much (most? all?) of the time.

Imagine if your dream life took another kind of form: instead of the visually based dreams you have now, they consisted of stories heard in the mind's ear—just as if someone were reading to you from a book. Suppose these auditory dreams had a certain degree of coherence and narrative force, as well as marked originality. It *might* be that your brain is producing them on the spot, with no planning or prior creative work. But surely it is far more likely that the stories were already formed before the reading began, stored in your brain for later enjoyment. This would be particularly true if the earlier parts of the story were clearly put there in anticipation of the later parts, thus indicating that the inner voice is not just making it up from moment to moment. In the same way, many dreams clearly proceed to a denouement that was decided from the outset—as with the typical anxiety dream that starts innocuously enough and then descends into fear and frustration. You are being *set up*. The idea that a dream is a moment-by-moment affair, concocted at the very time of telling, is surely not credible. Even the most fluent and practiced extemporary storyteller must do his preparation, must have his store of plots and characters, his dialogue skills—it doesn't all happen at the moment of telling. In the same way, the storyteller embedded in our unconscious dream machinery doesn't just make it all up on the spot: the narratives have already been laid down long before they reach the stage of constituting an occurring dream.

ORIGINALITY

If we think of dream construction on the model of moviemaking, we gain a sense of the complexity involved and of the interrelated skills that need to be brought to bear. I never cease to be amazed by the power and ingenuity of the individual image in a dream. In the case of photographic images, the camera simply records what is in front of it; but in the case of dream images, there is often no such original—the image is entirely created. You can have a dream image of something you have never seen the like of before. The closest analogue to this in film production is computer-generated imagery—and think how costly and complex that is! The brain must synthesize a brand-new dream image from basic raw materials, just as the computer technician must build a complex image from pixels. The latter takes a lot of time and advanced technology; the brain does it seemingly effortlessly, but behind the scenes the process must be just as sophisticated. Nor should we underestimate the ingenuity involved in matching feeling to form in dreams—that finely tuned harmony between the emotion in the dream and its visual expression. How does the brain manage to produce something so perfectly designed to express a certain feeling? It's a mixture of science and art that must surely astound us. That bathroom in my dream, with its fine sculptures and utter filth, combined the high and the low in an intensely memorable way. Set design in movies aims for just such evocative realism, such objectified affect; dreams are splendidly replete with it.

In this chapter I have described the dream-making process in anthropomorphic terms, as if a little homunculus (or team of homunculi) sits in the head and makes decisions in the way people making a movie do. This is helpful from an expository point of view, but for my harder-headed readers let me make it clear that I do not suppose that the brain really contains any such little guys. For such readers I could speak of cognitive modules, executive functions, and computational procedures—it would amount to the same, but now in the language of cognitive psychology and computer science. The basic point is that dream making must be conceived as a complex, temporally extended, multifaceted procedure, not as a simple spontaneous upsurge at the moment of dreaming. The film analogy is intended to make this conception vivid by isolating the functions and phases that must be involved. For my less pedantic readers, then, I will say that the brain contains its own miniature Hollywood, complete with producers, directors, actors, technicians, designers, wardrobe people, and hair stylists—and maybe even agents and publicists. And what counts as a box-office hit? The recurrent dream, of course, with its many sequels, and the blockbuster dream that lodges forever in the memory. Then there are the dreams that come and go, making little impression on us—as it were, the B movies and schlock staples of the dream world. All of them, however, have to be produced with intelligence, planning, and forethought. No dream is a simple reflex occurrence.

Seven

CINEMA AND HUMAN NATURE

MOVIE POWER

I began this book by inquiring into the power that movies have over the viewer, their psychological impact. In effect, the whole book has been an attempt to answer this question, by linking movies to some of our most basic natural traits. First, films engage our perceptual faculties in fundamental ways, particularly through the visual stance of looking *into* (chapter 2). We are predominantly visual creatures, perceptually, and movies amply reward our inquiring eyes, our insatiable desire to look and see. Second, they answer to our metaphysical status as psychophysical beings, the mind-body nexus that constitutes our nature; in particular, they play upon our ambivalent relationship to our own body (chapter 3). The screen is an arena in which our spiritual nature is foregrounded, the limpid pool of the screen recapitulating the transparency of consciousness. Thirdly, movies delve into our dreaming self, that submerged and seething alter ego that emerges when the sun goes down (chapters 4, 5, and 6). In the cinema we relive the life of the dreaming self.

Movies thus tap into the dreaming aspect of human nature. Moreover, they *improve* upon our dream life. They give us the dreams we yearn for. It is a rare individual who is not fascinated by his own dreams, with their raw ability to reveal, their magical expressiveness; movies partake in this fascination. The impact of movies stems, then, at least in part, from the primal power of the dream. To be sure, the dream component of the movie experience is augmented by the special qualities of the medium, but the primary emotional hook originates in the evocation of the dream.

INFLUENCE

To what extent do dreams themselves reflect our experience with movies? Granted the affinity I have been insisting upon, might it not be that what you dream is influenced by the films you have seen? Indeed, if the influence is strong and pervasive enough, might this not account for the analogies I have cited? Might it not be the case that movies resemble dreams because *our dreams have come to resemble movies*? This, of course, would undermine the argument I have been making, since it would locate the admitted similarities between dreams and movies in the fact that dreams are *shaped* by movies. The dream theory would come out as true, but trivially so. So let us consider whether such a position—the movie theory of dreams, as we might call it—has any plausibility.

The idea is that our dreams are essentially cultural products, shaped in their nature by the artifacts of society—in particular, films. We have internalized the film medium to such an extent that we literally screen inner movies in our sleep—the very forms of our dreams are derived from the forms we encounter in the cinema. This thesis, in its extreme form, is surely wildly implausible. What were people's dreams like before film came along? Were there perhaps no dreams then? Did film impose a form on dreams that they never had before? Do your dreams change their basic nature once you start watching films? The answer to these questions is surely no. Can we really suppose that in the early days of film everyone dreamed in black-and-white, with no voices? Then, with the advent of color, did they start to dream in brighter and more varied hues? What color were their dreams *before* black-and-white film? Nor would it be at all plausible to suppose that some of the central properties of dreams I identified in chapter 4—such as sensory/affective fusion and the blending of realism and fantasy—are by-products of cinema technology. These properties of dreams are surely ancient and hardwired. If an anthropologist told you that in some remote tribe people have dreams with sensory content but absolutely no emotional content, you would be rightly skeptical. Nor would you be very convinced if assured that in a saintly tribe somewhere safe from civilization no one ever dreams about himself. The suggestion that anxiety dreams began with industrialization would likewise leave you justifiably dubious.

We are not taught to dream, any more than we are taught to reach puberty; dreaming arises in our minds because of an inbuilt genetic program. The case is similar to what Noam Chomsky has long argued with respect to language: humans are born with an innate capacity for language that unfolds as the child progresses.[1] There are linguistic universals that transcend the particularities of culture, which are part of our biological nature. I suggest, similarly, that there are dream universals—such as sensory/affective fusion and egocentricity—that characterize all human dreamers. Dreaming is a matter of biology, not culture. Of course, as with language, the specific culture to which a person belongs contributes to the content of his or her dreams—you dream about what you have experienced and learned. What is innate and universal, however, are the basic structures of the dream, such as spatio-temporal discontinuity and object transformation. Eating is clearly an instinct, though what a person eats is determined by her culture; dreaming is an instinct too, though what a person dreams depends on her culture. So the fundamental structures of dreaming are not going to be affected by anyone's cultural exposure to movies or anything else. They are just not that plastic.

However, I don't wish to go to the opposite extreme and deny that movies make *any* contribution to our dream life. On the contrary, the marks of movies do sometimes show up in our dreams; and this is what we would expect if there exists a significant affinity between them. Dreams can contain what I shall call *cinematic flourishes.* For example, I recently had a dream about the death of a friend of mine, a distinguished philosopher I much admired. The dream was poignant in many ways, and appeared to suggest a wish to have spent more time with him, but it contained one very striking image: my friend's recently deceased body sitting in a chair, legs folded in contemplation, head lolling to one side, as if restfully. As I approached the body I noticed, as if in close-up, a cigar in his right hand (though he did not smoke), which had burned down close to his lifeless hand

and now supported an inch or so of teetering ash. This image, of the cigar lightly clasped in the fingers, still living, as it were, while its holder has expired, is a trope of the cinema that I have seen before. It really was as if the camera had swooped in close to reveal this poignant detail. This is what I mean by a cinematic flourish, a device from film that crops up in a dream. So I don't doubt that such local effects reflect the impact of cinema upon human dream life, and this kind of merging is exactly what the dream theory of movies would predict. What I doubt is the much more radical idea that the very architecture of dreams is simply a reflection of the movies we have seen.

CELEBRITY

We cannot avoid the question of celebrities. Actors appear in movies, playing characters; we see these actors, often again and again. Around the institution of film there have grown up ancillary institutions of celebrity, consisting of magazines, TV shows, online sites, and so on. Cults develop, fervor foments, and gods are born (and die). Two aspects of our relationship to celebrities stand out: a sense of familiarity and an attitude of worship. The attitude of worship reflects the manner in which stars are elevated to the status of Greek gods by the very medium in which they (or their flattened images) appear. But what accounts for the sense of familiarity, I think, is their assimilation to dream characters in the obscure recesses of our minds. For we dream about people we know. Friends and family are the primary dramatis personae of dreams—those with whom we are intimate. But if films approximate dreams, then it is *as if* we know the people who appear in them. If I am constantly seeing, say, Julia Roberts at the movies—getting close to her face, sensing her inward turmoil—I will automatically assign her to the cast of characters who populate my dreams: that is, my brain will tag her as an intimate. Why else is she in my dreams? Then I will have a strong impression that she and I are, well, *close.* Celebrity culture, then, trades upon this assimilation of film and dream, to create an impression (no doubt false) of intimacy. Who is a stalker stalking? Someone who features in her dreams, who else? If we end up literally dreaming about the star, then this line will become even further blurred. It will then be puzzling why the star does not know the fan: surely if I dream about someone, she should know who *I* am, because I typically dream about intimates of mine. The result is a confused and confusing state of mind.

As a footnote to this point, consider TV celebrities versus movie celebrities. TV celebrities seem to occupy a lower tier in the celebrity hierarchy than movie stars (though much higher than philosophy professors). The fantasies that surround them seem less potent. They are not deified in the same way. They seem, somehow, *smaller,* less radiant, less magnetic. We just don't feel the same *connection* to the stars of the small screen. Why? Because their medium doesn't mimic the dream in anything like the same way the film medium does. The absorption isn't there; the emotional hookup isn't anywhere near as pronounced; and the penetration into the psyche is nothing like as deep. Sure, TV celebrities have their ardent fans, but only movie stars reach the pantheon of the gods—which is really not so far removed from our own kitchen or living room. Movie stars are *family*. They have the supernatural sheen that rubs off from the movie screen, and the simple magnitude, but they are also part of our domestic dream life. They have a quotidian reality for us, as well as a godlike aura. The concept of a film star is thus confounding and crisscrossed—a mix of the sublime and the sublunary. (And what does the typical fan say, or scream, when confronted in the flesh by her film idol? Why, "Oh my god!" of course—as the mortal hand scrawls the illegible signature.) The movie star inspires a quite different constellation of attitudes and emotions from the TV star—the word itself seems out of place here.

PENETRATION

I have used the metaphor of penetration several times, to register the impact of movies on the mind. A well-known screenwriter of my acquaintance once remarked to me, in trying to express the particular power of cinema, that a good film "fucks you." It gets to your most private parts and gives you a good going over. Watching a movie is like having sex, with the movie as the dominant partner. Now I don't know how far to go with this lively metaphor, but it certainly captures some of the intimacy of the film experience, as well as its intrusive nature. When you open your consciousness to a movie, you are letting it enter your private space, where your sensitivities and vulnerabilities are located. The experience may be very good, even ecstatic, or it may be pretty damn bad. In either case, you have been penetrated. The dream is very similar: it is common to wake from a powerful dream as if you have been recently ravished. The dream will penetrate to your innermost being, leaving you feeling worked over, spent, sometimes resentful. Feeling fucked by a dream is nothing out of the ordinary.

I think this is the right way to think about the question of censorship and movie ratings. I don't intend here to make legislative recommendations, only to shed light on the particular receptivity that constitutes movie watching. When a child watches a film, his or her mind is open and susceptible, as it is in dreams. And just as a bad dream can shake a child profoundly, so can a film, if it pushes the right (or the wrong) buttons. The movie *The Ring* is a profoundly disturbing and scary film, despite the lack of sex and violence in it, uncannily achieving the condition of intense nightmare. I have no doubt that it absolutely terrified many thousands of children (it scared me quite a bit and I don't scare easily), and I wouldn't be surprised if it caused many a nightmare. Is this a good thing to do to kids? Yet it wasn't even rated R. The fixation on sex and violence in our society lets through films that can have a much larger impact on the psyche. A horror film can really get inside a child's mind, merging with his worst nightmares, creating intense anxiety and fear. This, at least, ought to be recognized. I had some sleepless nights as a child after watching horror films on TV that were much tamer than what is available now. Critical faculties are down while watching an absorbing film, as they are in dreaming, and the impact on the mind is correspondingly amplified. A steady diet of nightmares sounds to me like a bad regime in which to raise children. In any case, we should be aware that watching movies is a mentally invasive procedure. I have sometimes felt soiled by a film, as if I don't want it in my head and yet it is now in there (*Lethal Weapon 3* stands out in this category). The power of film to penetrate and linger is not to be denied.

PROPAGANDA

The power of film in creating propaganda should be seen in the same light. The critical faculties are reduced, the mind entering a state of dreamlike susceptibility and suggestibility—this is fertile ground for persuasion of one kind or another. Not for nothing have dubious (or worse) regimes used cinema to influence the attitudes of its people, the Nazi propaganda film being the most obvious example. Unflattering stereotypes can easily gain traction in this state of diminished critical thought; they can pass unhindered into the receptive recesses of the mind. Reading isn't so effective, because you can't read at all with your higher mental faculties turned off. But the base self, common to dreams and films, can be swayed by the moving image far more easily. Not that this power of film cannot be used for the good; but we should recognize that it is, not to put too fine a point on it, a type of mind fucking. It is getting to the soft core of the self, without the carapace of critical intelligence to protect it. (Imagine if *all* you had to go on in forming your beliefs and attitudes about the world were the contents of your dreams: you would end up with some very strange convictions about reality.) Film propaganda works because of the power of film to penetrate to our least rational side—the side so ruthlessly exploited by the dream.

ADVICE

What, then, is my advice to filmmakers? What should they do with the theories propounded in this book? Well, there is no straight deduction from these theories to a recipe for a successful film. That depends on far too many other factors. But some general guidelines suggest themselves. First, they should remember that their ultimate subject is the human soul, no matter what visual gimmickry adorns the screen. Everything about the medium points to the soul, as I argued in chapter 3. Even the most crass action sequence is meaningless unless the audience feels that human souls are in peril (mere robots getting blown up is no big deal). The eye might like to be dazzled, but the viewer is quickly bored if all the pyrotechnics have no psychological significance. It is the human soul as visually presented, to be sure, but it is still the interior that ultimately attracts our interest. An actor's body is merely the means she uses to put her mind on display. The screen must be seen as a container into which mentality is poured; it is not simply a showcase for shiny objects. (Even in the case of pornography states of mind matter, more so than is generally acknowledged.)

Secondly, movies are primarily a medium for sensation and feeling, not for abstract thought. Novels are constituted by words and sentences that express thoughts; how the words look on the page is not the point. The "intellectual novel" may or may not be a good idea, but the "intellectual film" is liable to fall flat. Adapting novels to the screen, then, involves a radical transformation in the artistic means employed, and a very good novel may well not translate into film at all successfully. Film enters the brain through its sensory centers and radiates outwards to the emotional sub-regions; film reception is not primarily a matter of forming *thoughts* about things. Film lives in the senses, not the intellect—which is not to say it cannot have serious themes. It must make contact with the emotions through its visual power (as well as through its soundtrack, which is not primarily a matter of words spoken but of sounds heard). A good filmmaker can make his images mesh seamlessly with the feelings expressed, just as a dream does this as a matter of course. *The Wizard of Oz,* which I have mentioned more than once, is a close-to-perfect film because it understands this so well: visually glorious, it weaves feeling into every image, just as in a dream—which, of course, it is. The story is simple, the characters well defined: it wafts through the mind like a light and airy dream (though with its dark moments). I think, too, that Jean Cocteau's *Beauty and the Beast* attains this dreamlike meshing of the visual and the emotional to an exceptional degree.

The right blend of realism and fantasy also maximizes the dreamlike character of a film, thus inducing that blissful state of dream immersion. A film must be rooted in reality, but it must also depart from reality and enter the realm of imagination. The best directors—Luis Buñuel, Alfred Hitchcock, David Lean, Stanley Kubrick, Steven Spielberg, and others—seem to me to recognize the essentially dreamlike character of the movie world, and they trade upon it in their films.

What is *A Clockwork Orange* but an audacious dream adventure insidiously combining nightmare and wish fulfillment?

THE FUTURE

Finally, let's indulge in a piece of science fiction. Suppose that movie technology progresses some time in the twenty-first century to the point that movies can be downloaded directly into the brain. You rent a cassette, plug it into your cortex, and enjoy the experience. There is no screen, no light projection—just mental images floating through your consciousness. Data is read off a disc and your neurons are appropriately stimulated. The movie has been rendered entirely mental. Your brain is directly caused to "screen" a purely inner movie. Then, supposing this, I want to make two observations. The first is that this strikes me as the manifest destiny of movies—the point toward which they are naturally moving. Who can doubt that if this technology became available it would be wildly popular? It would probably make obsolete the current formats for screening movies (just as the CD replaced vinyl records). Movies, as I noted in the previous section, are already partly mental products; so it seems only natural that they might eventually shed their material support and go completely mental.

The second observation—and my main point at the moment—is that it seems to me perfectly clear that such a movie format would *precisely* resemble the dream. The movie would consist of mental images arranged into a narrative sequence, and that is what a dream *is*. Images on the screen would be replaced with images in the mind, and with that the transition to dream would be complete. If movies took this form, it would hardly be necessary for me to write this book, because the thesis would seem so obviously true. But—to go back to my first point—this looks like the destiny of movies, their real underlying essence. They *want* to go radically inward. So the *ideal* movie is overtly dreamlike in its materials—a sequence of vivid mental images. Films aspire to the condition of dreams; this is what they dream of. These mind movies would directly mimic the dream state, despite the wakefulness of the "viewer," thus fulfilling the destiny inherent in the film medium from the start.

However, such a technology is a distant dream (as it were), since no one yet has any idea how to stimulate brain cells so as to produce specific images strung together into stories. It seems to me, though, to constitute the underlying essence of film—what it would be if only it knew how. This technology would extend, and possibly usurp, our natural dream life, allowing us to dream of whatever we liked whenever we wanted to. Dreams themselves would pale in comparison, especially artistically. I can imagine a whole race of people wanting to be plugged into mind movies all the time, consciously dreaming their lives away. Whether this would be a good thing, I shall not say; but given the power of movies so far, in their present relatively primitive state, you can see why it might be an irresistible temptation. Meanwhile, we will no doubt carry on letting old-fashioned movies made of splashes of two-dimensional light have their way with us.

REFERENCES

One THE POWER OF FILM

1. Cavell, *The World Viewed,* 164.
2. See McGinn, *The Mysterious Flame,* for a discussion of the mind-body problem.
3. For a critical discussion of this ideological approach to cinema see Carroll, *Mystifying Movies,* chapter 2.
4. See ibid., chapter 1, for a critical discussion.
5. Ibid., 29.
6. Ibid., chapter 5.

Two VISION AND THE SCREEN

1. Murch, *In the Blink of an Eye,* 122.
2. Ibid., 144.
3. See McGinn, *Mindsight,* chapter 3, for a discussion of this notion.
4. See Munsterberg, *The Photoplay,* and Arnheim, *Film as Art.*
5. See Kracauer, "The Establishment of Physical Existence," and Bazin, *What Is Cinema?,* vol. 1.
6. Bazin, *What Is Cinema?,* vol. 1, 96.
7. Ibid., 14.
8. Balazs, "The Close-Up," 256.
9. Ibid., 258.
10. Ibid., 260.
11. Mulvey, "Visual Pleasure and Narrative Cinema," 806.

Three THE METAPHYSICS OF THE MOVIE IMAGE

1. For a nice discussion of shadows see Casati, *The Shadow Club.*
2. This is a book that made a splash on its initial appearance, then disappeared from view for decades, and now once again is receiving its due.
3. Munsterberg, *The Photoplay,* 153–4.
4. Ibid., 133.
5. Ibid., 181.
6. Kawin, *Mindscreen,* 192.
7. Metz, "The Imaginary Signifier," 785.
8. Tyler, *Magic and Myth of the Movies,* 103.
9. Ibid., 93.
10. Ibid., 109.
11. Cavell, *The World Viewed,* 171–2.
12. Barthes, "The Face of Garbo," 650–1.
13. Arnheim, *Film as Art,* 67–8.
14. Andrew, *The Major Film Theories,* note 16, 257.
15. Tyler, *Magic and Myth of the Movies,* 31.
16. Arnheim, *Film as Art,* 36.
17. See McGinn, *The Mysterious Flame,* for a discussion of why it is surprising that flesh is the foundation of consciousness.
18. Barr, "CinemaScope: Before and After," 152.

Four DREAMS ON FILM

1. See McGinn, *Mindsight,* chapter 1, for a discussion.
2. Langer, *Feeling and Form,* 412.
3. Tyler, *Magic and Myth of the Movies,* 28.
4. Ibid., 195.
5. Arnheim, *Film as Art,* 21.
6. Murch, *In the Blink of an Eye,* 57–8.
7. Langer, *Feeling and Form,* 415.

8. See Eisenstein, *The Film Sense.*
9. See Pinker, *The Language Instinct.*
10. Miller, *Subsequent Performances,* 213–47.
11. Hobson, *Dreaming,* 59.
12. Ibid., 64.
13. Ibid., 113.
14. Quoted ibid., 22.
15. For a discussion, see Munsterberg, *The Photoplay,* 138.
16. See McGinn, *Mindsight,* chapters 6 and 7.
17. For a discussion of dream belief see ibid., chapter 7.
18. Freud, *The Interpretation of Dreams,* chapter 1.
19. Kracauer, "The Establishment of Physical Existence," 237.
20. Kawin, "The Mummy's Pool," 466–7.

Five REVIEWING THE DREAM THEORY

1. See also Hobson, *Dreaming,* chapter 7.

Six HOW TO MAKE A DREAM

1. See Pinker, *How the Mind Works,* chapter 4.
2. See Hobson, *Dreaming,* 28.

Seven CINEMA AND HUMAN NATURE

1. For a popular treatment see Pinker, *The Language Instinct.*

BIBLIOGRAPHY

Andrew, J. Dudley. *The Major Film Theories.* Oxford: Oxford University Press, 1976.

Arnheim, Rudolf. *Film as Art.* Berkeley: University of California Press, 1957.

Balazs, Bela. "The Close-Up." In Mast and Cohen, eds., *Film Theory.*

Barr, Charles. "CinemaScope: Before and After." In Mast and Cohen, eds., *Film Theory.*

Barthes, Roland. "The Face of Garbo." In Mast and Cohen, eds., *Film Theory.*

Bazin, André. *What Is Cinema?,* vol. 1. Berkeley: University of California Press, 1971.

Carroll, Noel. *Mystifying Movies: Fads and Fallacies in Contemporary Film Theory.* New York: Columbia University Press, 1988.

Casati, Roberto. *The Shadow Club.* New York: Knopf, 2003.

Cavell, Stanley. *The World Viewed.* Cambridge, Mass.: Harvard University Press, 1971.

Eisenstein, Sergei. *The Film Sense.* Translated by Jay Heyda. New York: Harcourt Brace & Company, 1947.

Freud, Sigmund. *The Interpretation of Dreams.* Translated by J. Strachey. New York: Avon, 1980.

Hobson, J. Allan. *Dreaming: An Introduction to the Science of Sleep.* Oxford: Oxford University Press, 2002.

———. *Dreaming as Delirium: How the Brain Goes Out of Its Mind.* Cambridge, Mass.: MIT Press, 1999.

Kawin, Bruce F. *Mindscreen: Bergman, Godard, and First-Person Film.* Princeton: Princeton University Press, 1978.

Kracauer, Siegfried. "The Establishment of Physical Existence." In Mast and Cohen, eds., *Film Theory.*

Langer, Suzanne K. *Feeling and Form.* New York: Charles Scribner's Sons, 1953.

Mast, Gerald, and Marshall Cohen, eds. *Film Theory and Criticism.* New York: Oxford University Press, 1985.

McGinn, Colin. *Mindsight: Image, Dream, Meaning.* Cambridge, Mass.: Harvard University Press, 2004.

———. *The Mysterious Flame.* New York: Basic Books, 2000.

Metz, Christian. "The Imaginary Signifier." In Mast and Cohen, eds., *Film Theory.*

Miller, Jonathan. *Subsequent Performances.* New York: Viking, 1986.

Mulvey, Laura. "Visual Pleasure and Narrative Cinema." In Mast and Cohen, eds., *Film Theory.*

Munsterberg, Hugo. *The Photoplay: A Psychological Study.* London: Routledge, 2002.

Murch, Walter. *In the Blink of an Eye.* 2nd ed. Los Angeles: Silman-James Press, 2001.

Pinker, Steven. *How the Mind Works.* New York: W. W. Norton & Company, 1999.

———. *The Language Instinct.* New York: William Morrow & Company, 1994.

Tyler, Parker. *Magic and Myth of the Movies.* London: Secker & Warburg, 1971.

About the Author

Colin McGinn was educated at Oxford University. In addition to his numerous articles for academic journals, McGinn has written extensively on philosophy and philosophers in such publications as *The New York Review of Books, London Review of Books, The New Republic,* and *The New York Times Book Review.* He is the author of sixteen previous books, including *The Mysterious Flame; Ethics, Evil, and Fiction; The Making of a Philosopher: My Journey through Twentieth-Century Philosophy; The Space Trap,* a novel; and his most recent, *Mindsight: Image, Dream, Meaning.* McGinn, who lives in New York City, is a professor of philosophy at Rutgers University and an avid water sports enthusiast who loves sailboarding and surfing.

A Note on the Type

The text of this book was set in Monotype Columbus, a contemporary face designed specifically for digital typesetting by Patricia Saunders. Named for Christopher Columbus, and released on the quincentenary of his 1492 voyage from Spain to the Americas, Monotype Columbus has a distinctly Spanish flavor to its letter forms. Saunders did, in fact, draw inspiration from fonts created by Jorge Coci in sixteenth-century Spain, as well as from italic fonts by the brilliant typographer, Robert Granjon, to create this lively and highly readable new face.

Composed by Creative Graphics,
Allentown, Pennsylvania

Printed and bound by R. R. Donnelley & Sons,
Harrisonburg, Virginia

Designed by M. Kristen Bearse

DATE DUE